Congressional Research Service

Agriculture-Based Biofuels: Overview and Emerging Issues

Randy Schnepf
Specialist in Agricultural Policy

May 1, 2013

Congressional Research Service

7-5700

www.crs.gov

R41282

CRS Report for Congress ————————————————
Prepared for Members and Committees of Congress

Summary

Since the late 1970s, U.S. policymakers at both the federal and state levels have authorized a variety of incentives, regulations, and programs to encourage the production and use of agriculture-based biofuels—i.e., any fuel produced from biological materials. Initially, federal biofuels policies were developed to help kick-start the biofuels industry during its early development, when neither production capacity nor a market for the finished product was widely available. Federal policy (e.g., tax credits, import tariffs, grants, loans, and loan guarantees) has played a key role in helping to close the price gap between biofuels and cheaper petroleum fuels. Now, as the industry has evolved, other policy goals (e.g., national energy security, climate change concerns, support for rural economies) are cited by proponents as justification for continuing or enhancing federal policy support.

The U.S. biofuels sector responded to these government incentives by expanding output every year from 1980 through 2011 (with the exception of 1996), with important implications for the domestic and international food and fuel sectors. Production of the primary U.S. biofuel, ethanol (derived from corn starch), has risen from about 175 million gallons in 1980 to nearly 14 billion gallons in 2011. U.S. biodiesel production (derived primarily from vegetable oil), albeit much smaller, has also shown strong growth, rising from 0.5 million gallons in 1999 to a record 969 million gallons in 2012. Despite the rapid growth of the past decades, total agriculture-based biofuels consumption accounted for only about 8% of U.S. transportation fuel consumption (9.7% of gasoline and 1.5% of diesel) in 2012.

Federal biofuels policies have had costs, including unintended market and environmental consequences and large federal outlays (estimated at $7.7 billion in 2011, but declining to $1.3 billion in 2012 with the expiration of the ethanol blender's tax credit). Despite the direct and indirect costs of federal biofuels policy and the relatively small role of biofuels as an energy source, the U.S. biofuels sector continues to push for federal involvement. But critics of federal policy intervention in the biofuels sector have also emerged. Current issues and policy developments related to the U.S. biofuels sector that are of interest to Congress include

- Many federal biofuels policies require routine congressional monitoring and occasional reconsideration in the form of reauthorization or new appropriations.

- The 10% ethanol-to-gasoline blend ratio—known as the "blend wall"—poses a barrier to expansion of ethanol use. The Environmental Protection Agency (EPA) issued waivers to allow ethanol blending of up to 15% (per gallon of gasoline) for use in model year 2001 and newer light-duty motor vehicles. However, the limitation to newer vehicles, coupled with infrastructure issues, could limit rapid expansion of blending rates.

- The slow development of cellulosic biofuels has raised concerns about the industry's ability to meet large federal usage mandates, which in turn has raised the potential for future EPA waivers of mandated biofuel volumes and has contributed to a cycle of slow investment in and development of the sector.

In 2012, the expiration of the blender tax credit, poor profit margins (due primarily to high corn prices), and the emerging blend wall limitation have contributed to a drop-off in ethanol production and have generated considerable uncertainty about the ethanol industry's future.

Contents

Figures

Tables

Contacts

Introduction

Increasing dependence on foreign sources of crude oil, concerns over global climate change, and the desire to promote domestic rural economies have raised interest in renewable biofuels as an alternative to petroleum in the U.S. transportation sector. However, energy from renewable sources has historically been more expensive to produce and use than fossil-fuel-based energy.[1] U.S. policymakers have attempted to overcome this economic impediment by enacting an increasing number of policies since the late 1970s, at both the state and federal levels, to directly support U.S. biofuels production and use. Policy measures have included blending and production tax credits to lower the cost of biofuels to end users, an import tariff to protect domestic ethanol from cheaper foreign-produced ethanol, research grants to stimulate the development of new technologies, loans and loan guarantees to facilitate the development of biofuels production and distribution infrastructure, and, perhaps most importantly, minimum usage requirements to guarantee a market for biofuels irrespective of their cost.[2]

This report describes agriculture-based biofuels and the evolution of the U.S. biofuels sector with a focus on the role that federal policy has played in shaping its development.[3] In addition, it highlights emerging issues that are critical to the biofuels sector and of relevance to Congress.

Biofuels Defined

Any fuel produced from biological materials—whether burned for heat or processed into alcohol—qualifies as a "biofuel." The term is most often used to refer to liquid transportation fuels produced from some type of biomass. The two principal biofuels are ethanol and biodiesel; however, other fuels such as methanol and butanol could also qualify when produced from a qualifying biomass.

Biomass is organic matter that can be converted into energy. Common examples of biomass include food crops, energy crops (e.g., switchgrass or prairie perennials), crop residues, wood waste and byproducts, and animal manure. The term biomass has been a part of legislation enacted by Congress for various programs over the past 30 years; however, its explicit definition has evolved with shifting policy objectives.[4] Over the last few years, the concept of biomass has grown to include such diverse sources as algae, construction debris, municipal solid waste, yard waste, and food waste. The exact definition of biomass is critical, since it determines which feedstocks and resultant biofuels qualify for the different federal biofuels programs.

For example, the principal biofuels program in effect as of this report is the Renewable Fuels Standard (RFS), which mandates annual usage rates for four nested categories of biofuels— (1) total renewable fuels, (2) advanced renewable fuels, (3) cellulosic biofuel, and (4) biomass-

---

[1] This excludes the costs of externalities (e.g., air pollution, environmental degradation, illness and disease, or indirect land use changes and market-price effects) linked to emissions associated with burning either fossil fuels or biofuels.

[2] For more details and a complete listing of federal biofuels programs and incentives, see CRS Report R42566, *Alternative Fuel and Advanced Vehicle Technology Incentives: A Summary of Federal Programs.*

[3] See the list of related CRS Reports available at the CRS website "Issues in Focus: Agriculture: Agriculture-Based Biofuels" including CRS Report R41985, *Renewable Energy Programs and the Farm Bill: Status and Issues.*

[4] See CRS Report R40529, *Biomass: Comparison of Definitions in Legislation Through the 112th Congress.*

based diesel.[5] Qualifying biofuels under each category are differentiated by their type of feedstock, the land on which the feedstock is produced (e.g., federal versus private, virgin versus previously cultivated soil, etc.), the production process used both to grow the feedstock and to process it into a biofuel (certain technologies are favored based primarily on environmental considerations), and the estimated amount of greenhouse gas emissions that result from the entire production pathway.

The idea of formally defining biomass has evoked criticism. Some argue that by explicitly enunciating qualifying feedstocks, the definition may be excluding new or as-yet-undiscovered feedstocks that may emerge in the future. Also, there appears to be some inconsistency across programs. For example, algae-based biofuels presently do not qualify for inclusion under the RFS cellulosic biofuels mandate, but do qualify for the "advanced other" biofuels mandate, as well as for the cellulosic biofuels tax credit and the depreciation allowance for qualifying cellulosic biofuels plants.[6] These differentiations tend to confuse and may slow or inhibit investments in algae-based biofuels.

Ethanol from Corn Starch Dominates U.S. Biofuels Production

Ethanol is the principal biofuel produced in the United States (**Figure 1**). Ethanol, or ethyl alcohol, is an alcohol made by fermenting and distilling simple sugars. As a result, ethanol can be produced from any biological feedstock that contains appreciable amounts of sugar or materials that can be converted into sugar such as starch or cellulose. Sugar beets and sugar cane are examples of feedstock that contain sugar. Corn contains starch that can relatively easily be converted into sugar. Trees, grasses, and most agricultural and municipal wastes are made up of a significant percentage of cellulose, which can also be converted to sugar, although with more difficulty than is required to convert starch.

Since its development in the late 1970s, U.S. biofuels output has relied almost exclusively on ethanol produced from corn starch. Small amounts of ethanol have also been produced using sorghum, wheat, barley, and brewery waste. This contrasts with Brazil, the world's second-largest ethanol producer behind the United States, where sugar cane is the principal feedstock. In 2012, the United States and Brazil accounted for 88% of the world's ethanol production.[7] Approximately 13.3 billion gallons of ethanol were produced in the United States in 2012, over 95% from corn starch.

Because of concerns over the significant expansion in corn production for use as an ethanol feedstock, interest has grown in spurring the development of motor fuels produced from cellulosic biomass materials. Since these biomass sources do not compete with traditional food and feed crops for prime cropland, it is thought that their use would result in substantially fewer unintended market effects. However, the technology needed for the conversion of cellulose into its constituent sugars before conversion to biofuels, while successful in laboratory settings, is thought to be expensive relative to corn ethanol and has yet to be replicated on a significant

---

[5] See CRS Report R40155, *Renewable Fuel Standard (RFS): Overview and Issues.*

[6] See CRS Report R42122, *Algae's Potential as a Transportation Biofuel.*

[7] According to data from the Renewable Fuel Association, U.S. ethanol production in 2012 was 13.3 billion gallons (61%), Brazil's was 5.8 billion gallons (27%), and the world total was 21.8 billion gallons (100%).

commercial scale.[8] Many uncertainties remain concerning both the viability and the speed of commercial development of cellulosic biofuels.[9]

Figure 1. Ethanol Had Nearly a 10% Share of U.S. Motor Gasoline Fuel Use in 2012

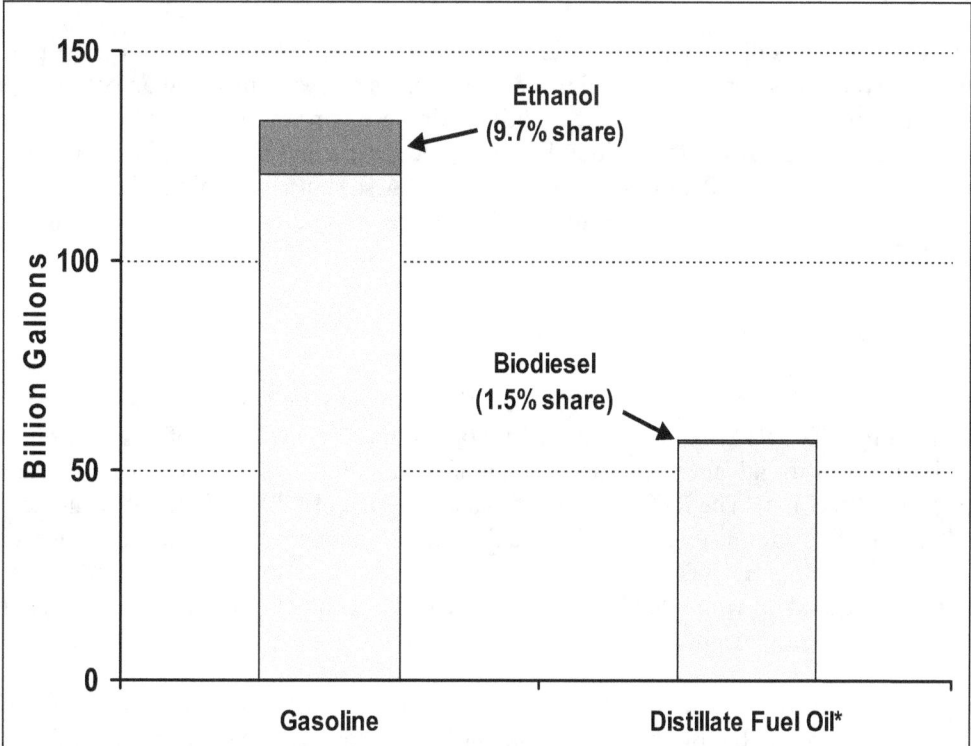

Sources: Calculated by CRS based on data from the Energy Information Agency (EIA), Department of Energy (DOE), *Monthly Energy Review*, March 2013: ethanol from Table 10.3, biodiesel from Table 10.4, and gasoline and distillate fuel oil use from Table 3.5.

Note: All data are in actual volumes; i.e., there is no conversion for gasoline energy equivalency. Distillate fuel oil includes both transportation and home heating oil uses.

After ethanol, biodiesel is the next most significant biofuel in the United States. Biodiesel is an alternative diesel fuel that can be produced from any type of organic-based oil, including vegetable oils, animal fats, and waste restaurant grease and oils. In the United States and Brazil, biodiesel has traditionally been made from soybean oil. In the European Union, rapeseed oil is the primary feedstock, while Canada relies primarily on canola oil. In recent years persistently high vegetable oil prices have pushed biodiesel producers to increase the share of much cheaper animal fats (especially poultry fat) and tropical palm oil; however, soybean oil remains the largest single source of biodiesel feedstock in the United States, with a share of over 56% in 2012.[10]

---

[8] In 2012, 20,069 gallons of cellulosic biofuels production were reported to the Environmental Protection Agency (EPA) under its RFS2 EMTS Informational Data system, at http://www.epa.gov/otaq/fuels/rfsdata/. Data concerning cellulosic biofuels production costs is proprietary and has not been made publicly available.

[9] See CRS Report R41106, *Meeting the Renewable Fuel Standard (RFS) Mandate for Cellulosic Biofuels: Questions and Answers*.

[10] Energy Information Agency (EIA), *Monthly Biodiesel Production Report*, U.S. Dept. of Energy (DOE), March 2013.

Other biofuels with the potential to play a role in the U.S. market include diesel fuel substitutes and other alcohols (e.g., methanol and butanol) produced from biomass.

Biofuels Value Determinants

The value of a biofuel is determined by its end use. Ethanol is primarily used as a substitute for gasoline; however, it has some additional properties (i.e., as an oxygenate and an octane enhancer) that provide value as a gasoline additive. Biodiesel's primary use is as a substitute for petroleum-based diesel transportation fuel; however, biodiesel can also be used as a direct substitute for home heating oil and as a blend in jet fuel. Also, both ethanol and biodiesel may derive additional value as an additive to meet federal usage mandates under the Renewable Fuel Standard (RFS) depending on market conditions.

The Renewable Fuel Standard (RFS)[11]

The RFS requires the blending of renewable fuels (including ethanol and biodiesel) in U.S. transportation fuel. The RFS includes specific quotas for total renewable biofuels, as well as nested subcategories for advanced biofuels (i.e., non-corn-starch ethanol), cellulosic biofuels, and biomass-based diesel fuel. The RFS also includes a cap on the eligible volume of corn-starch ethanol.[12] The RFS is administered by EPA. Qualifying biofuels must meet explicit criteria on lifecycle greenhouse gas (GHG) emissions[13] and feedstock production pathways (including restrictions on the land on which feedstocks are produced, feedstock production methods, and the biofuels plant processing technology).

Federal policy that mandates the use of a minimum volume of biofuel creates a source of demand that is not based on price, but rather on government fiat. As long as the consumption of biofuels is less than the mandated volume, its use is obligatory.

Ethanol Sources of Demand

With respect to ethanol, there is no difference to the end user between corn-starch ethanol, sugarcane ethanol, and cellulosic ethanol, although their production processes differ substantially in terms of feedstock, technology, and cost. As a result, all three share the same value determinants. In the presence of government policy, demand for ethanol derives from four potential uses:

- as an oxygenate additive in gasoline to help improve engine combustion and cleaner burning of fuel;

- as an additive to gasoline to enhance its octane level and engine performance;[14]

---

[11] The RFS referred to as RFS1 was begun by the Energy Policy Act of 2005 (§1501; P.L. 109-58). A greatly expanded RFS (referred to as RFS2) was established by the Energy Independence and Security Act of 2007 (EISA, §202, P.L. 110-140). For more information on the RFS, see CRS Report R40155, *Renewable Fuel Standard (RFS): Overview and Issues*; this is described in greater detail later in this report, in the section titled "Evolution of the U.S. Ethanol Sector."

[12] Each RFS biofuel category has an identifier code associated with it: D6 is for an unspecified renewable fuel, D5 is for an advanced biofuel, D4 is for biomass-based diesel, D3 is for cellulosic biofuel, and D7 is for cellulosic diesel.

[13] CRS Report R40460, *Calculation of Lifecycle Greenhouse Gas Emissions for the Renewable Fuel Standard (RFS)*.

[14] Ethanol's use as an additive for octane or oxygenate purposes occurs primarily at low blend levels of up to 5%, and (continued...)

- as an additive to gasoline at blend ratios of up to 10% ethanol and 90% gasoline (known as E10), to meet federally mandated minimum usage requirements under one of the RFS categories for qualifying ethanol biofuels;[15] or

- as a substitute for gasoline at ethanol-to-gasoline blend ratios greater than E10.

Biodiesel Sources of Demand

In the presence of government policy, demand for biodiesel derives from the following potential uses:

- as a substitute for petroleum-based diesel transportation fuel;

- as a substitute for home heating oil;

- as a blend in jet fuel; and

- as an additive to petroleum-based diesel to meet federally mandated minimum usage requirements under one of the RFS categories for qualifying biofuels.[16]

Biofuel Supply Relative to RFS Mandates Affects Valuation

Depending on the relationship between the RFS mandate (blending demand) and the available supply (production plus imports) of qualifying biofuels, different RFS biofuels categories may have significantly different valuations, as greater scarcity will lead to greater value.

Under the RFS, each gallon of qualifying biofuel has an associated renewable identification number (RIN) that is detached at point of blending and submitted to the EPA as proof of fulfilling that year's RFS usage requirement for a specific biofuel category.[17] When a specific biofuel is blended (or used) in excess of its RFS mandate, the surplus RINs may be sold (ideally to another fuel blender to make up for a shortfall in meeting that blender's own RFS mandate) or stored for use in meeting the following year's RFS mandate. As a result of their tradability, secondary markets for RINs—by RFS category—have developed and gain in importance whenever the supply of a specific biofuel type tightens relative to its RFS mandate. RIN values are nested— since cellulosic and biomass-based diesel RINs can be used to meet their own category as well as

---

(...continued)

is small relative to the growth in total usage of recent years. When ethanol is being added to enhance engine performance rather than as a fuel extender, it is a complement to gasoline and may potentially capture a price premium over standard gasoline.

[15] Because the RFS categories are nested, their values will include a premium to reflect a higher nesting. For example, corn ethanol only qualifies for the total renewable fuel category (D6). Ethanol from other feedstock qualifies for the more restrictive advanced biofuel category (D5) as well as the D6 category. Cellulosic ethanol also qualifies for the cellulosic biofuels category (D3) along with the D5 and D6 categories. Thus, as long as the RFS mandate is binding, a gallon of cellulosic ethanol will have inherently greater value than a gallon of advanced biofuel which itself has inherently greater value than a gallon of corn ethanol.

[16] Biodiesel qualifies for the biomass-based diesel (BBD) category (D4) which, by its nested nature, also qualifies for the advanced (D5) and total biofuel (D6) categories. If BBD is produced under a production process that uses cellulosic biomass as its originating feedstock, then it may be defined as cellulosic diesel (D7) and qualify for the nested cellulosic biofuels category (D3).

[17] RINs are discussed in more detail in CRS Report R40155, *Renewable Fuel Standard (RFS): Overview and Issues* and CRS Report R42824, *Analysis of Renewable Identification Numbers (RINs) in the Renewable Fuel Standard (RFS)*.

the advanced and total categories, they have an inherent premium over advanced and total RINs. Similarly, advanced RINs would have a premium over total RINs.

In contrast, when the supply of a specific biofuels category exceeds its mandated usage volume, the associated "nested" value will diminish. In volumes above the RFS total renewable mandate, biofuels use is no longer obligatory and it must compete directly in the marketplace with its petroleum-based counterpart. As a result, once they have met their RFS blending mandates, fuel blenders, seeking to maximize their profits, are very sensitive to price relationships between petroleum-based fuels and biofuels. This is particularly important for ethanol since it contains only about 68% of the energy content of gasoline. As a result, value-conscious consumers could be expected to willingly pay only about 68% of the price of gasoline for ethanol.

From 2006—when the RFS was first introduced—through 2011, both ethanol production capacity, supply (production and imports combined), and consumption have easily exceeded the federally mandated usage levels (**Figure 2**).[18] As a result, ethanol's marginal value during that period was as a transportation fuel (rather than as an additive), where it competed directly with gasoline. However, economic conditions changed substantially in 2012, driven largely by the severe drought that summer, and the RFS has played a larger role in driving ethanol use. As for biodiesel, which is significantly more expensive to produce than its petroleum-based counterpart, biodiesel's use has been driven almost entirely by federal policy—i.e., the RFS biomass-based diesel and the biodiesel production tax credit (described below).

Blend Wall Emerges as Major Value Determinant

An important valuation concern for U.S. ethanol consumption in 2013 is the emergence of the so-called "blend wall" as a constraint on domestic consumption of ethanol in sufficient volumes to satisfy the RFS mandate. Ethanol-gasoline blends of up to 10% ethanol are compatible with existing vehicles and infrastructure (fuel tanks, retail pumps, delivery infrastructure, etc.). All automakers that produce cars and light trucks for the U.S. market warranty their vehicles to run on gasoline with up to 10% ethanol (E10); however, automakers have been reluctant to offer such warranties for higher ethanol blend ratios. As a result, the 10% blend ratio represents an upper bound (sometimes referred to as the "blend wall") to the amount of ethanol that can be introduced into the gasoline pool given the current automobile fleet and fuel delivery infrastructure.

In 2012, ethanol accounted for nearly a 10% share of blended gasoline sold in the United States (**Figure 1**). In 2013, the RFS mandates for non-advanced ethanol of 13.8 bgals will likely exceed the blend wall (estimated at approximately 13 bgals by CRS based on EIA data). Supplementing actual ethanol blending with carry-over RINs (estimated at 2.6 bgals) will likely be sufficient to satisfy the 2013 RFS; however, surmounting the blend wall could prove more difficult in 2014.[19] Because of this infrastructure constraint, ethanol production in excess of the blend wall will have limited value in the domestic market unless it is consumed at higher blending ratios in flex-fuel vehicles (FFVs) or exported into the international market.[20]

---

[18] The exception is cellulosic ethanol, whose RFS mandate was waived to lower levels by EPA in each of its first four years of existence (2010-2013).

[19] Scott Irwin and Darrel Good, "Freeze It—A Proposal for Implementing RFS2 through 2015" *farmdoc-Daily*, April 10, 2013.

[20] For a discussion of the blend wall and associated policy and market issues, see CRS Report R40155, *Renewable Fuel Standard (RFS): Overview and Issues*.

Figure 2. U.S. Corn Ethanol Consumption, RFS, and Blend Wall, 1980 to 2022

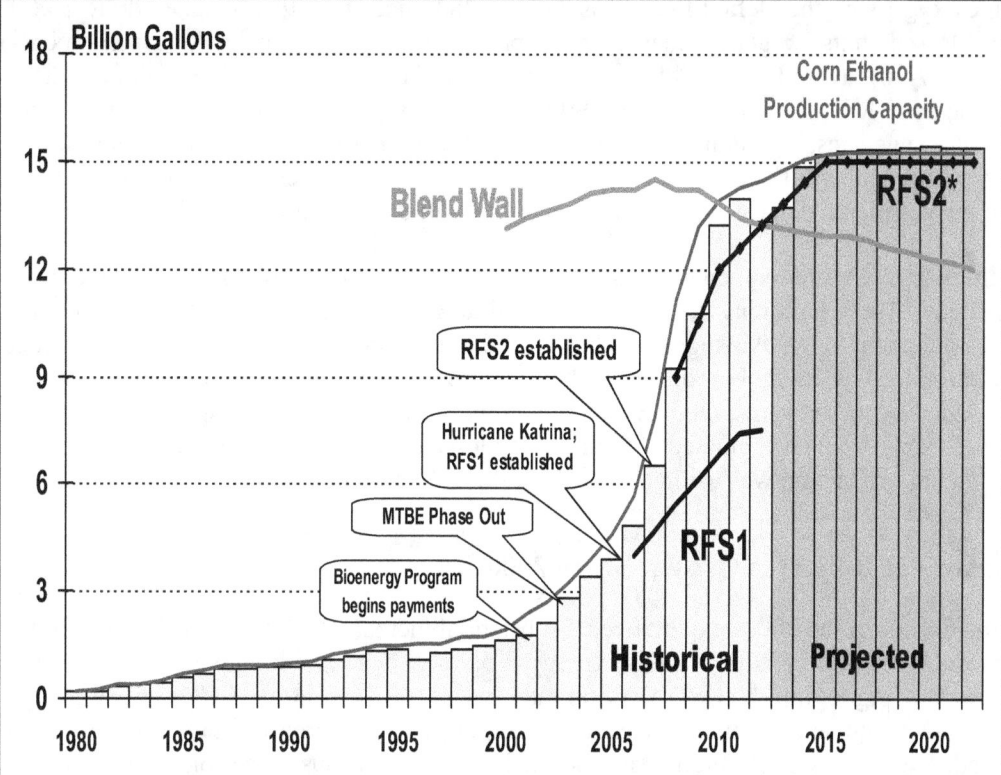

Source: Ethanol consumption historical data for 1980-2012 is from EIA, *Monthly Energy Review*, March 2013, Table 3.5; blend wall historical and projected data are calculated by CRS based on the EIA, DOE, data found in the AEO *Annual Energy Outlook* 2013. Projections for 2013-2022 are corn ethanol production from FAPRI, *FAPRI-MU Biofuel Baseline*, FAPRI-MU Report #02-13, March 2013. The projection data exclude ethanol production from advanced sources, e.g., cellulosic or sugarcane.

Note: RFS2* shown in the chart represents the non-advanced component (RFS code D6) equal to the total renewable fuel mandate minus the advanced biofuel mandate, and roughly approximates the cap on qualifying corn-starch ethanol consumption; ethanol from advanced sources are excluded from this data and this chart. Achieving the corn ethanol consumption levels in excess of the blend wall (as portrayed in this chart and described later in the text) would necessitate substantial consumption at higher blends such as E15 or E85.

Evolution of the U.S. Ethanol Sector

Federal Policy Kick-Starts Ethanol Production

Several events contributed to the startup and growth of U.S. ethanol production in the late 1970s. First, the global energy crises of the early and late 1970s provided the rationale for a federal policy initiative aimed at promoting energy independence from foreign crude oil sources. In response, the U.S. Congress established a partial exemption for ethanol from the motor fuels excise tax (legislated as part of the Energy Tax Act of 1978). All ethanol blended in the United States—whether imported or produced domestically—was eligible for a $0.40 per gallon tax credit. In 1980, an import duty for fuel ethanol was established by the Omnibus Reconciliation Act of 1980 (P.L. 96-499) to offset the domestic tax credit being applied to foreign-sourced ethanol.

As U.S. ethanol production began to emerge in the 1980s, ethanol became recognized as a gasoline oxygenate. The Deficit Reduction Act of 1984 raised the ethanol tax credit to $0.60 per gallon.[21] Based on its oxygenate characteristic, provisions of the Clean Air Act Amendments of 1990 (CAAA90) favored ethanol blending with reformulated gasoline (RFG).[22] One of the requirements of RFG specified by CAAA90 was a 2% oxygen requirement, which was met by blending "oxygenates," including methyl tertiary butyl ether (MTBE) and ethanol into the gasoline.[23] Ethanol was the preferred oxygenate in the Midwest where it was produced, while MTBE—a petroleum derivative—was used in almost all RFG outside of the Midwest.

In addition to CAAA90 oxygenate requirements, a tax credit for small ethanol producer was established in 1990 (Omnibus Budget Reconciliation Act of 1990; P.L. 101-508) as a $0.10 per gallon supplement to the existing ethanol tax credit, but limited to the first 15 million gallons of ethanol produced by ethanol producers with production capacity below 30 million gallons per year.[24] Aided by these events, the U.S. ethanol industry steadily grew during its first two decades—rising from an estimated 175 million gallons in 1980 to 1.8 billion gallons in 2001, when ethanol production was using about 7% of the U.S. corn crop.

Government Role Has Grown Since 2000

The first decade of the 2000s experienced a substantial increase in federal involvement in the U.S. biofuels sector. In FY2001, the Bioenergy Program[25] began making payments from the U.S. Department of Agriculture's (USDA's) Commodity Credit Corporation (CCC)[26] to eligible biofuel producers—ethanol and biodiesel—based on any year-to-year increases in the quantity of biofuels produced. The Bioenergy Program was instituted by USDA because the program's principal goal was to encourage greater purchases of eligible farm commodities used in the production of biofuels (e.g., corn for ethanol or soybean oil for biodiesel).

The executive order creating the Bioenergy Program was followed by a series of legislation containing various provisions that further aided the U.S. biofuels industry. The first of these new laws—the Biomass Research and Development Act of 2000 (Biomass Act; Title III, P.L. 106-224)—contained several provisions to expand research and development in the area of biomass-based renewable fuel production.

---

[21] "Ethanol Policy: Past, Present, and Future," by James A. Duffield, Irene M. Xiarchos, and Steve A. Halbrook, *South Dakota Law Review*, Fall 2008.

[22] USDA, Office of Energy Policy and New Uses, *The Energy Balance of Corn Ethanol: An Update*, AER-813, by Hosein Shapouri, James A. Duffield, and Michael Wang, July 2002.

[23] "Status and Impact of State MTBE Ban," Energy Information Administration (EIA), U.S. Dept. of Energy (DOE), revised March 27, 3003; available at http://www.eia.doe.gov/oiaf/servicerpt/mtbeban/.

[24] The 30 million gallon threshold was extended to 60 million gallons by the Energy Policy Act of 2005 (P.L. 109-58).

[25] The Bioenergy Program was initiated on August 12, 1999, by President Clinton's Executive Order 13134. On October 31, 2000, then-Secretary of Agriculture Glickman announced that, pursuant to the executive order, $300 million of Commodity Credit Corporation (CCC) funds ($150 million in both FY2001 and FY2002) would be made available to encourage expanded production of biofuels.

[26] The CCC is a U.S. government-owned and -operated corporation, created in 1933, with broad powers to support farm income and prices and to assist in the export of U.S. agricultural products. Toward this end, the CCC finances USDA's domestic farm commodity price and income support programs and certain export programs using its permanent authority to borrow up to $30 billion at any one time from the U.S. Treasury.

The 2002 farm bill (P.L. 107-171) included several biofuels programs spread across three separate titles—Title II: Conservation, Title VI: Rural Development, and Title IX: Energy (the first-ever energy title in a farm bill). Each title contained programs that encouraged the research, production, and use of renewable fuels such as ethanol, biodiesel, anaerobic digesters, and wind energy systems. In addition, Section 9010 of Title IX codified and extended the Bioenergy Program and its funding by providing that $150 million would be available annually through the CCC for FY2003-FY2006.[27]

The Healthy Forests Restoration Act of 2003 (P.L. 108-148) amended the Biomass Act of 2000 by expanding the use of grants, contracts, and assistance for biomass to include a broader range of forest management activities. It also expanded funding availability of programs established by the Biomass Act and the 2002 farm bill, and it established a program to accelerate adoption of biomass-related technologies through community-based marketing and demonstration activities, and to establish small-scale businesses to use biomass materials.

The American Jobs Creation Act of 2004 (P.L. 108-357) contained a provision (Section 301) that replaced the existing tax exemptions for alcohol fuels (i.e., ethanol) with an excise tax credit of $0.51 per gallon. This act also extended the small ethanol producer tax credit.

MTBE Phase-Out Enhances Ethanol's Value

In addition to a growing list of federal and state policies, the U.S. biofuels industry received an additional boost in the early 2000s with the emergence of water contamination problems associated with underground MTBE storage tanks in several locations scattered throughout the country. MTBE was thought to be a possible carcinogen and, as a result, posed serious health and liability issues. In 1999, California (which, at the time, consumed nearly 32% of the MTBE used in the United States) petitioned the U.S. Environmental Protection Agency (EPA) for a waiver of the CAAA90 oxygenate requirement.[28] However, California's waiver request was denied by the EPA in mid-2001 since the EPA determined that there was sufficient ethanol production available to replace MTBE.

By 2003, legislation that would phase out or restrict the use of MTBE in gasoline had been passed in 16 states, including California and New York (with a combined 40% national MTBE market share).[29] Between October 1, 2003, and January 1, 2004, over 43% of MTBE consumption in the United States was banned. According to the EIA, the state MTBE ban would require an additional demand for ethanol of 2.73 billion gallons in 2004.

With the legislative boosts and the MTBE phase-out, investments in the biofuels sector began to show results. The number of plants producing ethanol grew from 50 on January 1, 1999, to 81 by January 1, 2005. Concomitantly, U.S. ethanol production began to accelerate, rising to 3.9 billion gallons by 2005 and using over 14% of the nation's corn crop (**Table 1**), up from 1.8 bgals and 7% of the corn crop in 2001.

---

[27] The Bioenergy Program was phased out at the end of FY2006.

[28] "Status and Impact of State MTBE Ban," Energy Information Administration (EIA), U.S. Dept. of Energy (DOE), revised March 27, 3003; available at http://www.eia.doe.gov/oiaf/servicerpt/mtbeban/.

[29] Ibid.

Table 1. U.S. Corn-Use Share of Annual Production by Major Activity, 1980 to 2012

Period	Ethanol	Food	Exports	Feed
1980-1984	2%	11%	30%	64%
1985-1989	4%	14%	26%	46%
1990-1994	5%	14%	21%	58%
1995-1999	5%	14%	21%	55%
2000-2004	10%	14%	18%	60%
2005-2009	25%	11%	18%	55%
2010-2012	41%	12%	12%	37%

Source: Period averages are calculated by CRS from the USDA, PSD database, March 8, 2013.

Note: Values may sum to greater than 100% because some usage may derive from carryover stocks. The table data for the "Feed" and "Export" categories have not been adjusted to include distillers dried grains and solubles (DDGS)—a protein-rich animal feed that is a by-product of corn-based ethanol production.

The Ethanol Industry's Perfect Storm in 2005

On the heels of the large MTBE phase-out that occurred in 2004 and the surge in ethanol demand, two major events coincided in 2005 to produce extremely favorable economic conditions in the U.S. ethanol sector that persisted through most of 2006. These events included the following.

- The Energy Policy Act of 2005 (EPACT; P.L. 109-58) was signed into law on August 8, 2005. EPACT contained several provisions related to agriculture-based renewable energy production, including biofuels research and funding, expansions of existing biofuels tax credits and creation of new credits, and the creation of the first-ever national minimum-usage mandate, the Renewable Fuels Standard (RFS1; Section 1501), which required that 4 billion gallons (bgals) of ethanol be used domestically in 2006, increasing to 7.5 bgals by 2012.

- In August and September 2005, Hurricanes Katrina and Rita struck the Gulf Coast region causing severe damage to local petroleum importing and refining infrastructure, putting them off-line for several months, and driving gasoline prices sharply higher. Meanwhile, corn prices remained relatively low at about $2 per bushel, creating a period of extreme profitability for the ethanol sector.

The combination of high ethanol prices and relatively low corn prices that began in late 2005 and persisted through 2006 and into 2007 created a period of "unique" profitability for the U.S. ethanol industry (**Figure 3**). At that time, a 40 million gallon nameplate ethanol plant costing approximately $60 million could recover its entire capital investment in less than a year of normal operations.[30] In addition, the establishment of the first RFS—by guaranteeing a market for new ethanol production—removed much of the investment risk from the sector.

---

[30] Based on CRS simulations of an ethanol dry mill spreadsheet model developed by D. Tiffany and V. Eidman in *Factors Associated with Success of Fuel Ethanol Producers*, Staff Paper P03-7, Dept of Applied Economics, University of Minnesota, August 2003. Note, nameplate capacity represents the capacity that the design engineers will warrant. In most cases, an efficiently run plant will operate in excess of its nameplate capacity.

Figure 3. Comparison of Monthly Prices: Ethanol versus Corn

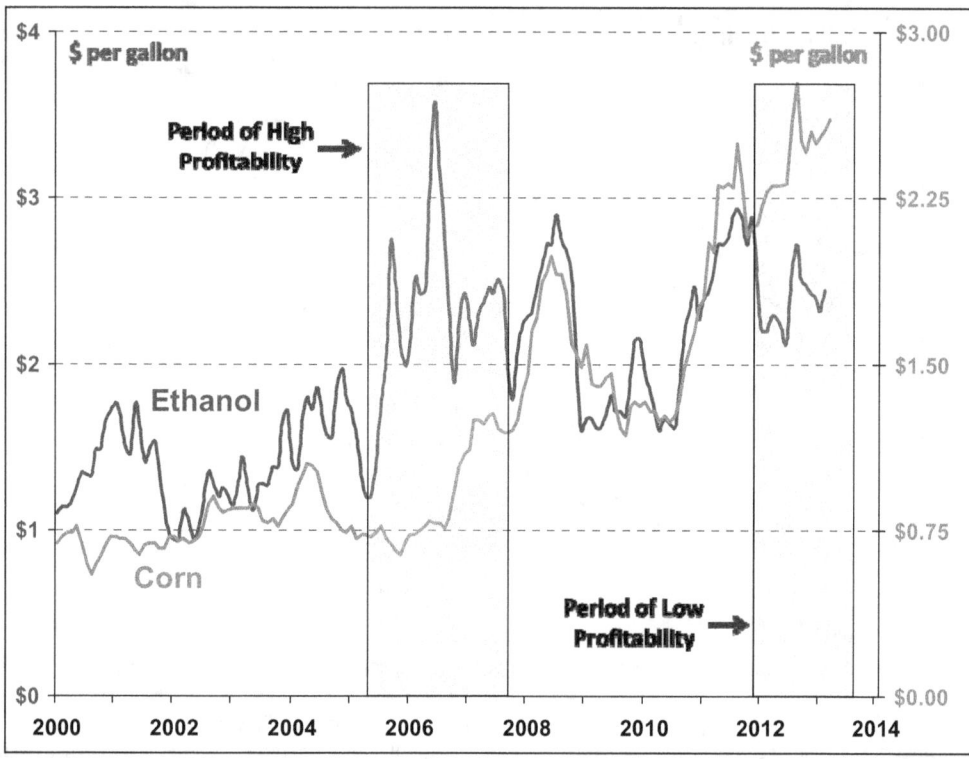

Source: Corn price data are monthly average farm prices, National Agricultural Statistics Service (NASS), USDA; ethanol price is the rack price, f.o.b., Nebraska Ethanol Board, Nebraska Energy Office, Lincoln, NE.

Note: Corn prices ($ per bushel) have been converted to $ per gallon by CRS—i.e., the price of corn used per gallon of ethanol—by dividing the per bushel price by 2.75 (an estimate of gallons of ethanol per bushel of corn).

As a result of this "perfect storm" of policy and market events, investment money flowed into the construction of new ethanol plants, and U.S. ethanol production capacity (either in existence or under construction) more than doubled in just four years, rising from an estimated 4.4 bgals produced in 81 plants in January 2005 to 10.6 bgals produced in 170 plants by January 2009. The ethanol expansion was almost entirely in dry-mill corn processing plants. As a result, corn's role as the primary feedstock used in ethanol production in the United States continued to grow. In 2006, corn use for ethanol nearly matched U.S. corn exports at about 2.1 billion bushels. In 2007, U.S. corn exports hit a record 2.4 billion bushels; however, by then corn-for-ethanol use had jumped to over 3 billion bushels. For the first time in U.S. history, the bushels of corn used for ethanol production would be greater than the bushels of corn exported (**Table 1** and **Figure 4**).

EISA Greatly Expands Mandate, Shifts Focus to Cellulosic Biofuels

In light of the rapid expansion of the U.S. biofuels industry, the RFS1 mandate was outgrown in 2006—the same year it was first implemented (**Figure 2**). On December 19, 2007, Congress dramatically raised the "bar" by passing the Energy Independence and Security Act of 2007 (EISA, P.L. 110-140).[31] EISA superseded and greatly expanded EPACT's biofuels mandate relative to historical production (**Figure 5**).

---

[31] See CRS Report R40155, *Renewable Fuel Standard (RFS): Overview and Issues*.

Figure 4. Annual U.S. Corn Use by Major Activity, 1980 to 2012

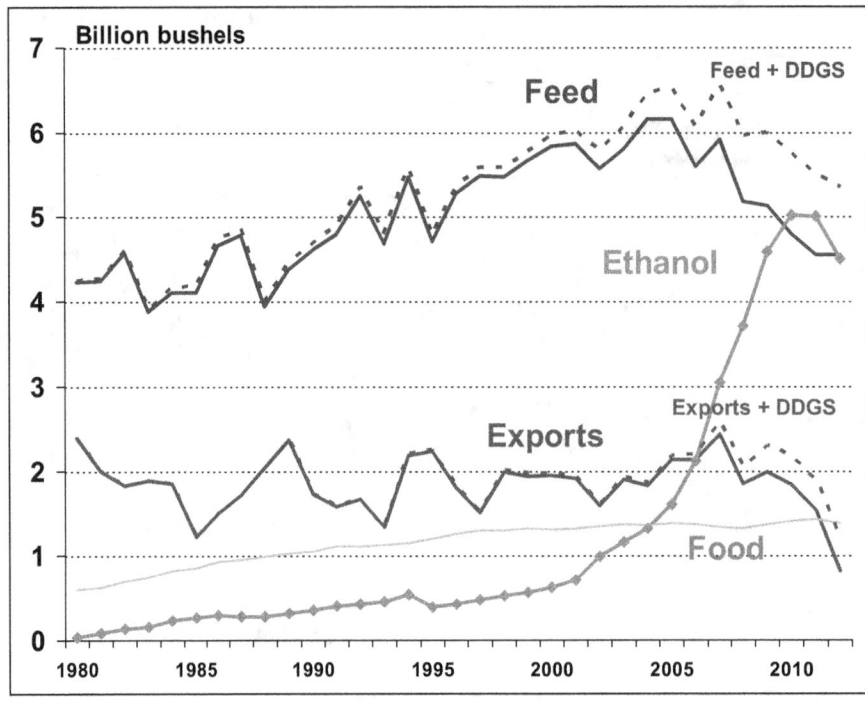

Source: USDA, Production, Supply, and Distribution (PSD) database, March 8, 2013.
Notes: Feed includes a residual category to balance USDA supply and demand estimates. The corn-to-ethanol production process generates a co-product, DDGS, which is a protein-rich animal feed. Both "Feed" and "Export" categories have been adjusted to include DDGS, as shown by the dotted lines.

Figure 5. Renewable Fuels Standard (RFS2) vs. U.S. Ethanol Production Since 1995

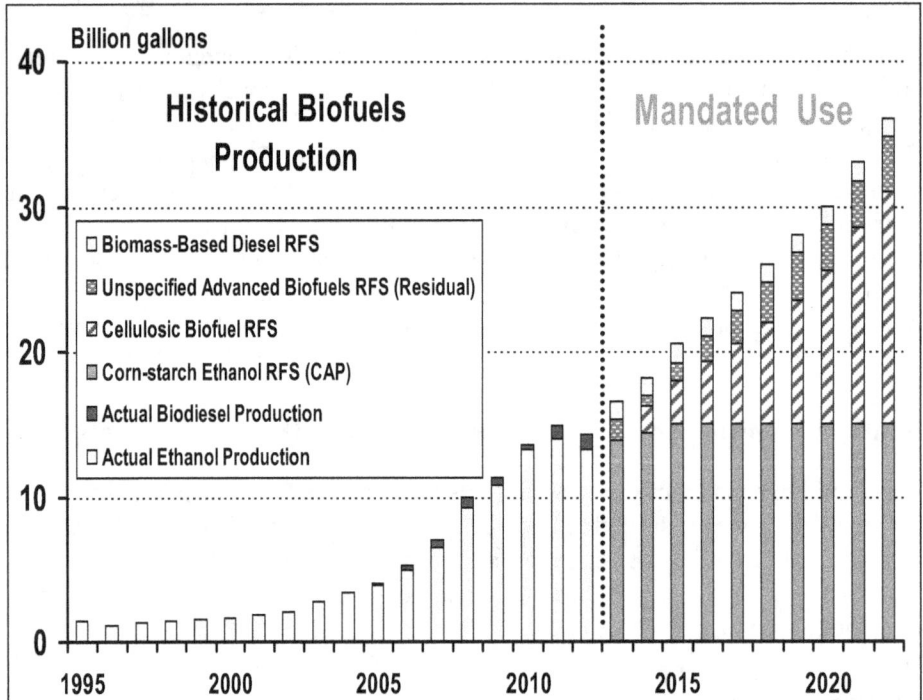

Sources: Actual ethanol production data for 1995-2012 is from Renewable Fuels Association; data for RFS2 mandates is from EISA (P.L. 110-140). Data includes proposed revision to RFS2 cellulosic mandate for 2013.

The expanded RFS (referred to as RFS2) required the use of 9 bgals of biofuels in 2008 and expanded the mandate to 36 bgals annually in 2022. The new mandate had some provisos, foremost of which was that only 15 bgals of annual RFS-qualifying biofuels could be ethanol from corn starch. As a result, all increases in the RFS mandate from 2016 onward must be met by advanced biofuels (i.e., non-corn-starch biofuels) and no less than 16 bgals must be derived from cellulosic feedstock in 2022. In addition, the new mandate established by EISA carved out specific volume requirements for biomass-based diesel fuels.

Meanwhile, prices for many agricultural commodities—including nearly all major U.S. program crops—started a steady upward trend in late 2006. Then, in early 2007, the upward trend for commodity prices turned into a steep rise. By mid-2008 market prices for several agricultural commodities had reached record or near-record levels (**Figure 6**).[32] In particular, both corn and crude oil hit record high prices in both spot and futures markets, thus symbolizing the growing linkage between U.S. field crops and energy markets.[33]

Figure 6. Monthly Price Indexes for Corn, Soybeans, and Crude Oil, 2000 to 2013

(nominal monthly prices are indexed such that 2006 = 100)

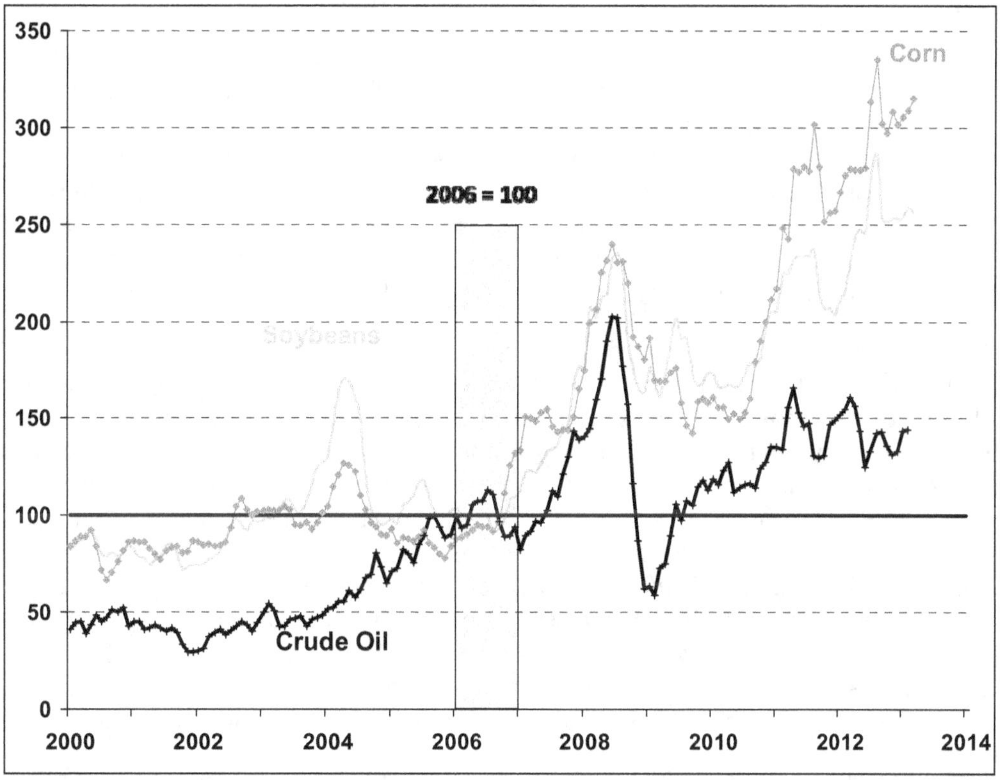

Sources: Corn and soybean prices are monthly average farm prices (MAFPs), National Agricultural Statistics Service (NASS), USDA; crude oil is the spot price, f.o.b., for West Texas Intermediate, Cushing, OK, EIA, DOE.
Notes: To facilitate comparison of relative price movements, the monthly prices have been converted by CRS to an index where the 12-month average for calendar 2006 has been set to 100.

---

[32] For more information about markets during this period, see CRS Report RL34474, *High Agricultural Commodity Prices: What Are the Issues?* See also, "What Is Driving Food Prices," by Philip C. Abbott, Christopher Hurt, and Wallace E. Tyner, Farm Foundation, July 2008; hereinafter referred to as Abbott et al., 2008.

[33] On June 23, 2008, the nearby futures contract for No. 2, yellow corn hit a then-record $7.65 per bushel on the Chicago Board of Trade. On July 7, 2008, the nearby futures contract for Crude Oil hit $147.27 per barrel at the New York Mercantile Exchange, while the nearby Brent Crude Oil contract hit $147.50 at the ICE Futures Europe exchange.

The upward rise in the price of corn in 2007 and early 2008 sucked the profits out of the U.S. biofuels sector and put the brakes on new investment (**Figure 3**). It also fueled a "food-versus-fuel" debate about the potential for continued expansion in corn use for ethanol to have unintended consequences in other agricultural and environmental markets. While most economists and market analysts agreed that the dramatic price rise of 2008 was due to factors other than biofuels policy, they also are nearly universally agreed that the strong, steady growth in ethanol demand for corn has had an important and sustained upward price effect, not just on the price of corn, but in other agricultural markets including food, feed, fuel, and land.

By mid-2008, the commodity price rise had completely reversed itself and turned into a near free-fall, coinciding with the global financial crisis that broke in late 2008.[34] The extreme price volatility created many difficulties throughout the marketing chain for agricultural buyers and sellers. The experience of $7.00-per-bushel corn, albeit temporary, shattered the idea that biofuels were a panacea for solving the nation's energy security problems and left concerns about the potential for unintended consequences from future biofuels expansion.

2008 Farm Bill Reinforces Focus on Cellulosic Biofuels

The 2008 farm bill (Food, Conservation, and Energy Act of 2008; P.L. 110-246) extended and expanded many existing biofuels programs.[35] In particular, Title XV ("Trade and Tax Provisions") extended the biofuels tax incentives and the tariff on ethanol imports, although the tax credit for corn-starch ethanol was reduced to $0.45 per gallon. But in the wake of the commodity market price run-up of early 2008, the new farm bill also re-emphasized EISA's policy shift towards research and development of advanced and cellulosic bioenergy in an effort to avoid many of the unintended consequences of relying too heavily on major field crops as the principal biomass feedstock. In addition, it established a new tax credit of $1.01 per gallon for cellulosic biofuel.

Like the 2002 farm bill, it contained a distinct energy title (Title IX) that covers a wide range of energy and agricultural topics with extensive attention to biofuels, including corn starch-based ethanol, cellulosic ethanol, and biodiesel. Energy grants and loans are provided through initiatives such as the Bioenergy Program for Advanced Biofuels to promote the development of cellulosic biorefinery capacity. The Repowering Assistance Program supports increasing efficiencies in existing refineries. Programs such as the Rural Energy for America Program (REAP) assist rural communities and businesses in becoming more energy-efficient and self-sufficient, with an emphasis on small operations. Cellulosic feedstocks—for example, switchgrass and woody biomass—are given high priority both in research and funding. The Biomass Crop Assistance Program (BCAP), the Biorefinery Assistance Program, and the Forest Biomass for Energy Program provide support to develop alternative feedstock resources and the infrastructure to support the production, harvest, storage, and processing of cellulosic biomass feedstocks.

Title VII, the research title of the 2008 farm bill, contains numerous renewable-energy-related provisions that promote research, development, and demonstration of biomass-based renewable energy and biofuels. One of the major policy issues debated prior to the passage of the 2008 farm bill was the impact of the rapid, ethanol-driven expansion of U.S. corn production. This issue was made salient by the dramatic surge in commodity prices experienced in 2007 and early 2008. In partial consideration, the enacted bill requires reports on the economic impacts of ethanol

---

[34] Permanent Subcommittee on Investigations, U.S. Senate, *Wall Street and the Financial Crisis: Anatomy of a Financial Collapse*, Majority and Minority Staff Report, April 13, 2011.

[35] See CRS Report R41985, *Renewable Energy Programs and the Farm Bill: Status and Issues*.

production, reflecting concerns that the increasing share of corn production being used for ethanol contributed to high commodity prices and food price inflation.

However, funding authority for Title IX bioenergy programs was fairly limited—about $1 billion in mandatory funding and only slightly more than $100 million in discretionary funding was actually available during the life of the 2008 farm bill (FY2008-FY2012). In addition, all of the major Title IX bioenergy programs expired at the end of FY2012 and lacked baseline funding going forward. The 2008 farm bill (including Title IX) was extended through FY2013 by the American Taxpayer Relief Act (ATRA; P.L. 112-240).[36] However, all major bioenergy provisions of Title IX—with the exception of the Feedstock Flexibility Program for Bioenergy Producers—have no new mandatory funding in FY2013 under the ATRA farm bill extension.

Questions Emerge Concerning Rapid Biofuels Expansion

By 2009, more than half of all U.S. gasoline contained some ethanol (mostly blended at the 10% level or lower). However, national gasoline transportation fuel consumption peaked in 2007 at about 142.5 bgals and has been steadily declining—driven by a weak economy and improving passenger vehicle fuel economy. In 2010 U.S. ethanol consumption reached an estimated 12.9 billion gallons (bgals), which was blended into roughly 138 bgals of gasoline—this represents about 9.3 % of annual gasoline transportation demand on a volume basis.[37]

Meanwhile, robust economic growth in major global markets in 2010 and early 2011 (including China, India, Brazil, and other parts of Asia and the Middle East) reinvigorated international consumer demand and, when coupled with a weak U.S. dollar and events that occurred in international feed grain markets—drought in Russia, Kazakhstan, and the Ukraine in 2010, plus strong Chinese demand for corn and feedstuffs—contributed to record U.S. agricultural export values in 2010 and 2011 and helped to push commodity prices, especially corn, upward again.[38]

By 2010, U.S. ethanol production consumed 40% of the U.S. corn crop and surpassed corn-for-feed use for the first time in history (**Figure 4**). Combined strong demand from export markets and ethanol contributed to near historic low ending stock projections (relative to expected demand) for U.S. corn and soybean for 2010 and 2011.[39] These market conditions helped to spur another surge in agricultural commodity prices starting in mid-2010 (**Figure 6**), thus spreading the effects of rapidly expanding ethanol production and corn demand across several other sectors of the U.S. economy as well.

In addition to expanding domestic production of biofuels, there has been some interest in expanding imports of sugar-based ethanol—usually produced from sugar cane in Brazil—to help satisfy the RFS for advanced biofuels.[40] U.S. sugar-ethanol imports peaked at 660 million gallons in 2006 (including 434 million from Brazil). Market factors in 2010-2012—U.S. ethanol production approaching the "blend wall", high international sugar prices, lower-than-expected sugarcane output in Brazil, and a weak U.S. dollar—resulted in the United States becoming a net exporter of ethanol during those years (**Figure 7**).[41]

---

[36] See the section "2008 Farm Bill Expiration" later in this report for details.

[37] EIA, DOE, "Petroleum Products Supplied by Type;" http://www.eia.gov/totalenergy/data/monthly/pdf/sec3_15.pdf.

[38] USDA, ERS, *Outlook for U.S. Agricultural Trade*, AES-72, November 30, 2011.

[39] For more information on this and other market factors, see CRS Report R41956, *U.S. Livestock and Poultry Feed Use and Availability: Background and Emerging Issues*.

[40] And to help satisfy California's Low Carbon Fuel Standard (LCFS) described later in this report.

[41] Based on official statistics from the International Trade Commission, Dept. of Commerce.

Figure 7. Annual U.S. Ethanol Exports and Imports Since 1990

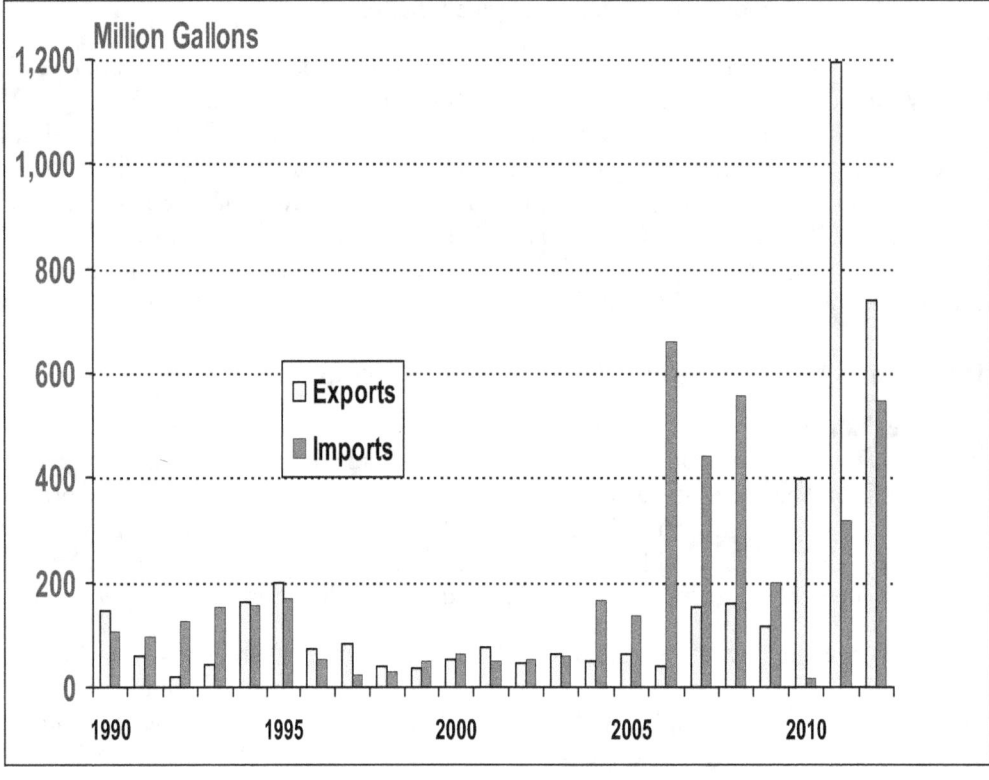

Source: U.S. Department of Commerce, U.S. Census Bureau, Foreign Trade Statistics.

Severe Drought Across Much of Corn Belt Slows Ethanol Industry

In early 2012, high market prices and nearly ideal springtime planting conditions across much of the United States led to substantial and extensive early corn planting. On June 12, 2012, USDA projected U.S. corn plantings of 95.9 million acres—the most since 1937. Normal weather patterns were expected to produce a record 2012 corn harvest of 14.8 billion bushels, which in turn would lead to a build-up in U.S. corn ending stocks in 2013 of nearly 2 billion bushels (up 111% year-to-year), and a 2012/2013 season-average corn price of $4.60/bushel (down 25%).[42] A record harvest and return to low corn prices were eagerly anticipated by both the ethanol and livestock industries.

However, in mid-June, an extensive swath of the Central and Southern Plains and much of the Corn Belt were hit by a combination of extreme heat and dryness that produced what was referred to as a "flash drought." By August 2012—just two months after its optimistic forecast of May— USDA had completely reversed its outlook from one of abundance to one of shortage. USDA lowered its forecast for U.S. corn production to 10.8 billion bushels (a 27% drop of 4 billion bushels from its May forecast), corn price projections were raised sharply to $8.20 per bushel (up 78%), and stocks of feed grains and soybeans were forecast to approach historic low levels relative to demand by the end of 2012/2013 crop year (i.e., at the end of summer 2013).[43]

---

[42] Midpoint of a projected range of $4.20 to $5.00 per bushel, *World Agricultural Supply and Demand Estimates (WASDE)*, World Agricultural Outlook Board (WAOB), USDA, June 12, 2012.

[43] *WASDE*, WAOB, USDA, August 10, 2012.

Market prices for ethanol were not able to keep up with escalating production costs (primarily for corn) and negative production margins resulted in the idling of several ethanol facilities (**Figure 3**). As a result, U.S. ethanol production in 2012 declined to 13.3 billion gallons—the first decline in production since 1996, when then-record corn prices temporarily set back ethanol production. The outlook for low corn supplies until the 2013 corn harvest in the September-November period is expected to dampen ethanol production in 2013 as well, possibly reducing it below the 2012 level.[44]

RIN Prices Rise Sharply in Early 2013

Despite waning ethanol production, RFS mandates for biofuel use continued to grow in 2013 to 16.55 bgals of total biofuels, including 2.75 bgals advanced biofuels and a residual 13.8 bgals for corn ethanol. In contrast, national transportation consumption of gasoline-type fuels, which had hit its peak in 2007 at about 142.5 bgals, was projected at slightly under 131 bgals in 2013, with an implied ethanol blend wall of about 13 bgals.[45]

The price for renewable identification numbers (RINs)[46] for basic renewable ethanol (D6)—as reported from thinly traded markets[47]—soared from under $0.05 per gallon during most of 2012 to over $1.00 per gallon in early March 2013.[48] As a result, the RIN values for a fuel blender blending 1 million gallons of E10 (using 100,000 gallons of ethanol) in 2012 might have been $5,000 based on an average ethanol RIN price of about $0.05. The hypothetical value implied for that same volume at $1 per RIN would be $100,000.

The rapid RIN price increase is linked to the impending collision of the RFS mandates and the ethanol blend wall, which, without rapid expansion of the E15 or E85 markets, will likely require the use of accumulated RIN stocks for mandate compliance in 2013 and 2014.

Uncertainties Cloud Biofuels Future

In addition to the ethanol blend wall, the expanded RFS2 is likely to play a dominant role in the development of the U.S. biofuels sector, but with considerable uncertainty regarding spillover effects in other markets and on other important policy goals.[49] The rapid expansion of U.S. corn ethanol production and the concomitant dramatic rise in corn use for ethanol—USDA estimates that over 40% of both the 2011 and 2012 U.S. corn crops was used for ethanol production—has

---

[44] Informa projects that U.S. ethanol production will fall by nearly 550 million gallons to 2013, to a level of 12.8 billion gallons—Informa Economics, "Retail Gasoline Price Impact of Compliance with the Renewable Fuel Standard," whitepaper prepared for the Renewable Fuel Association, March 25, 2013.

[45] EIA, *Monthly Energy Review*, March 2013; at http://www.eia.gov/totalenergy/data/monthly/#renewable.

[46] RINs are 38-character numeric and alpha codes generated when a qualified renewable fuel is produced or imported that move through the supply chain with the renewable blendstock and are transferred to buyers, either with physical biofuel or separated from it, as a credit. RINs are the basic currency for compliance and trades in the Renewable Fuels Standard. In RIN trade, D6 RINs for ethanol and D4 RINs for biomass diesel or biodiesel get the most attention because they are the most liquid. For information on RINs, see CRS Report R40155, *Renewable Fuel Standard (RFS): Overview and Issues* and CRS Report R42824, *Analysis of Renewable Identification Numbers (RINs) in the Renewable Fuel Standard (RFS)*.

[47] OPIS Ethanol and Biodiesel Information Service, U.S. RINs (prices in U.S. $/RIN), Ethanol & Gasoline Component Spot Market Prices, various weekly issues, January-March 2013.

[48] Scott Irwin and Darrel Good, "Exploding Ethanol RINs Prices: What's the Story?," *FarmdocDaily*, Department of Agriculture and Consumer Economics, University of Illinois, March 8, 2013, at http://farmdocdaily.illinois.edu/.

[49] See CRS Report R40155, *Renewable Fuel Standard (RFS): Overview and Issues*.

provoked questions about its long-run sustainability and the possibility of unintended consequences in other markets as well as for the environment.[50] Policymakers and the U.S. biofuels industry also are confronted by questions regarding the ability to meet the expanding RFS mandate for biofuels from non-corn sources such as cellulosic biomass materials, whose production capacity has been slow to develop,[51] or biomass-based diesel, which remains expensive to produce owing to the relatively high prices of its feedstocks.

It is widely believed that the ultimate success of the U.S. biofuels sector will depend on its ability to shift away from traditional row crops such as corn or soybeans for processing feedstock, and toward other, cheaper forms of biomass—such as prairie grass or algae—that do not compete with traditional food crops for land and other resources. Recent federal biofuels policies have attempted to assist this shift by focusing on the development of a cellulosic biofuels industry.[52] However, the speed of cellulosic biofuels development remains a major uncertainty, since new technologies must first emerge and be implemented on a commercial scale. The uncertainty surrounding the development of such new technologies and their commercial adaptation has been a major impediment to the flow of much needed private-sector investment funds into the cellulosic biofuels sector.

Ethanol Production Capacity Centered in Corn Belt

As of April 8, 2013, U.S. ethanol production was underway or planned in 210 plants located in 28 states based primarily around the central and western Corn Belt, where corn supplies are most plentiful (**Table 2** and **Figure 8**). Existing U.S. ethanol plant capacity was estimated at 14.763 billion gallons per year (BGPY), with another 0.158 BGPY of capacity under construction (either as new plants or expansion of existing plants). Thus, total annual U.S. ethanol production capacity in existence or under construction was about 14.9 BGPY, well in excess of the 13.8 bgals RFS2 corn-starch ethanol residual quota for 2013 (**Figure 2**).

Table 2. U.S. Ethanol Output and Production Capacity by State

| Rank | State | # of Plants | Operating Production | | | Current Nameplate Capacity (MGPY) | Under Contr. or Expansion (MGPY) |
			MGPY	% of output	Cumulative % output		
1	Iowa	41	3,903	30%	30%	3,908	—
2	Nebraska	27	1,509	11%	41%	1,822	—
3	Illinois	14	1,413	11%	52%	1,454	—
4	Minnesota	22	1,110	8%	60%	1,225	—
5	S. Dakota	15	1,016	8%	68%	1,016	—
6	Indiana	14	947	7%	75%	1,136	—
7	Wisconsin	9	504	4%	79%	504	5

[50] See CRS Report R40155, *Renewable Fuel Standard (RFS): Overview and Issues.*

[51] See CRS Report R41106, *Meeting the Renewable Fuel Standard (RFS) Mandate for Cellulosic Biofuels: Questions and Answers.*

[52] Cellulosic biofuels are derived from the sugar contained in plant cellulose. For more information, see CRS Report R41106, *Meeting the Renewable Fuel Standard (RFS) Mandate for Cellulosic Biofuels: Questions and Answers.*

Rank	State	# of Plants	Operating Production			Current Nameplate Capacity (MGPY)	Under Contr. or Expansion (MGPY)
			MGPY	% of output	Cumulative % output		
8	Ohio	7	478	4%	82%	538	—
9	Kansas	13	386	3%	85%	507	45
10	N. Dakota	4	360	3%	88%	360	—
11	Michigan	5	268	2%	90%	268	—
12	Tennessee	2	225	2%	92%	225	—
13	Missouri	6	210	2%	93%	271	—
14	Texas	4	205	2%	95%	355	—
15	New York	2	164	1%	96%	164	—
	Others (13)	25	506	4%	100%	1,010	108
U.S. Total		**210**	**13,203**	**100%**		**14,763**	**158**

Source: Renewable Fuels Association as of April 8, 2013; state-level aggregations are by CRS and include several approximations of current plant operating levels.

Note: Output and production capacity data are in million gallons per year (MPGY).

Figure 8. U.S. Ethanol Production Capacity Is Centered on the Corn Belt

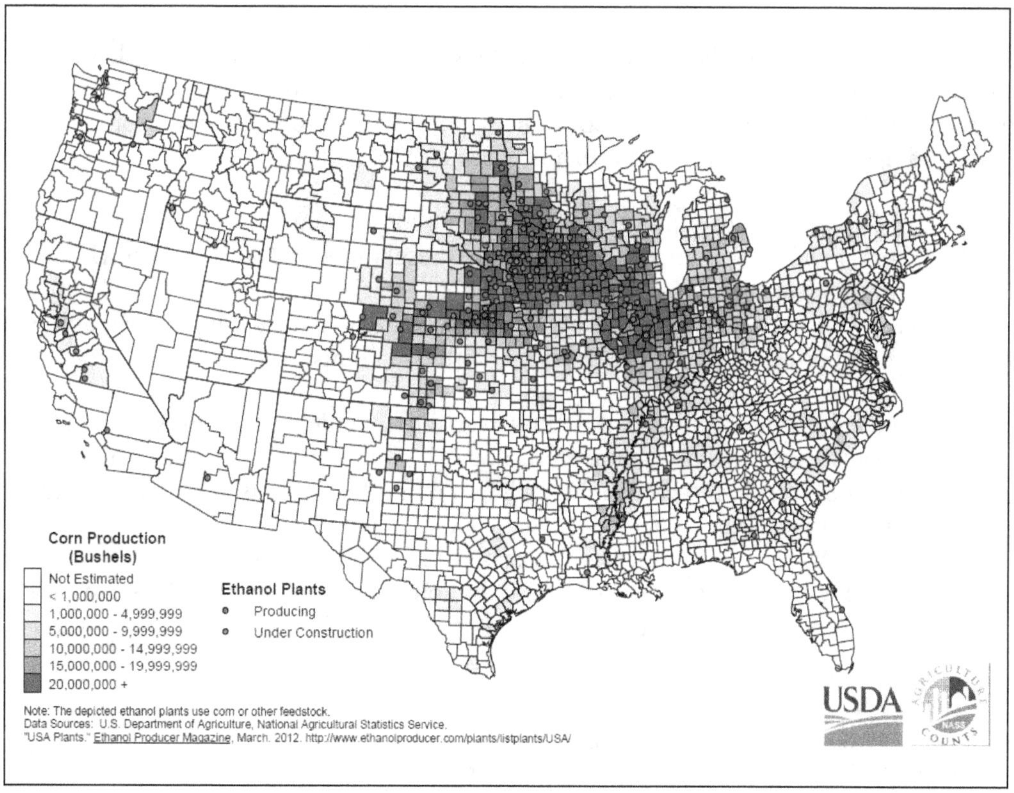

Source: USDA; U.S. corn production for 2011 compared with ethanol plant locations as of March 8, 2012; available at http://www.nass.usda.gov/Charts_and_Maps/Ethanol_Plants/U._S._Ethanol_Plants/index.asp.

Iowa is by far the leading ethanol-producing state, with a 30% share of total U.S. output. The top six Corn Belt states of Iowa, Nebraska, Illinois, Minnesota, South Dakota, and Indiana account for nearly 75% of national production (**Table 2**). On a national level, actual operating capacity of 13.2 BGPY represents about 89% of nameplate capacity. This is because several states, including Nebraska, Minnesota, Indiana, Kansas, Ohio, and the "other" category of states, are operating substantially below their nameplate capacity, suggesting that poor industry profitability has been widespread across the country, primarily due to high feedstock cost and limited availability.

Evolution of the U.S. Biodiesel Sector

Biodiesel can be produced from any animal fat or vegetable oil (such as soybean oil or recycled cooking oil). Historically, most U.S. biodiesel was made from soybean oil. As a result, U.S. soybean producers and the American Soybean Association (ASA) are strong advocates for greater government support for biodiesel production. However, with the rise in soybean prices since 2007 (**Figure 6**), biodiesel producers have aggressively shifted to cheaper vegetable oils and animal fats (especially poultry fat), such that by 2011 nearly 44% of U.S. biodiesel production was estimated to be based on sources other than soybean oil.[53] In recent years, many ethanol production facilities have added technology to remove corn oil from distillers grains and solubles, thus generating an additional income stream to help offset depressed profit margins.[54] The corn oil produced by this "end-stream" technology is typically not suitable for the food industry. Instead, the main uses of this added corn oil has been as an energy supplement in livestock and poultry rations, and for biodiesel production.

According to the National Biodiesel Board (NBB), biodiesel is nontoxic, biodegradable, and essentially free of sulfur and aromatics. In addition, it works in any diesel engine with few or no modifications and offers similar fuel economy, horsepower, and torque, but with superior lubricity and important emission improvements over petroleum diesel.[55]

To date, biodiesel is used almost uniquely as a substitute for petroleum diesel transport fuel. Biodiesel delivers slightly less energy than petroleum diesel (about 92%); however, U.S. biodiesel consumption remains small relative to national diesel consumption levels. In 2012 (**Figure 1**), U.S. biodiesel consumption represented about 1.5% (in diesel-equivalent units) of national diesel transportation fuel use of about 46.8 billion gallons.[56]

Biodiesel is compatible with existing petroleum-based diesel vehicles and infrastructure (fuel tanks, retail pumps, delivery infrastructure etc.) such that biodiesel does not face a blend wall similar to ethanol. As a result, the potential blending pool for biodiesel is significantly larger than just the transportation diesel fuel market. Because biodiesel and diesel fuel are so similar, biodiesel can also be used for the same non-transportation activities—the two largest of which are home heating and power generation. In 2012, 53.2 billion gallons of diesel fuel were used for heating and power generation by residential, commercial, and industry, and by railroad and vessel

---

[53] EIA, *Monthly Biodiesel Production Report*, DOE, March 2013.

[54] Robert Wisner, "Feedstocks Used for U.S. Biodiesel: How Important is Corn Oil?" *AgMRC Renewable Energy & Climate Change Newsletter*, April 2013, at http://www.agmrc.org.

[55] For more information, visit the NBB at http://www.biodiesel.org.

[56] EIA, DOE; biodiesel production estimates from "Annual Energy Outlook 2013," Transportation Sector Energy Use by Mode and Type, Reference Case.

traffic, bringing total U.S. diesel fuel use to nearly 106.7 billion gallons (including 46.8 billion gallons of transportation fuel use and 6.8 billion gallons of residual fuel oil).

Fuel blenders and consumers are very sensitive to price differences between biodiesel and petroleum-based diesel. The price relationship between vegetable oils and petroleum diesel is the key determinant of profitability in the biodiesel industry—about 7.5 pounds of vegetable oil are used in each gallon of biodiesel. Since late 2010, soybean oil prices have averaged over $0.50/lb. such that the vegetable oil feedstock component of biodiesel has cost over $3.75/gal. Additional processing and marketing costs likely push wholesale biodiesel prices into the $4.50/gal. to $5.00/gal. range compared with petroleum diesel wholesale prices of $3.05/gallon during that period. As a result, the biodiesel industry has depended on federal support—especially the production tax credit and the RFS for biomass-based diesel—for its economic survival.

Federal Programs Help Kick-Start U.S. Biodiesel Production

The U.S. biodiesel industry did not emerge until the late 1990s. In 1999, U.S. biodiesel production was still less than 1 million gallons. Bioenergy Program payments provided an initial impetus for biodiesel plant investments from 2001 through 2006. The American Jobs Creation Act of 2004 (P.L. 108-357) created the first ever federal biodiesel tax incentive—a federal excise tax and income tax credit of $1.00 for every gallon of agri-biodiesel (i.e., virgin vegetable oil and animal fat) that was used in blending with petroleum diesel; and a $0.50 credit for every gallon of non-agri-biodiesel (i.e., recycled oils such as yellow grease). The distinction between biodiesel from virgin and recycled oils was eventually removed (P.L. 110-343; October 3, 2008), and all biodiesel qualified for the credit of $1.00 per gal.

Starting in late 2005 through 2006, the U.S. biodiesel industry received a major economic boost from the same series of market and policy developments described for ethanol—i.e., high petroleum prices and low agricultural commodity prices.[57] Soybean oil prices were still relatively low priced during the 2000 through 2006 period, when they averaged $0.21/lb. (this compares with an average of nearly $0.44/lb. since 2007). The Energy Policy Act of 2005 extended the biodiesel tax credit and established a Small Agri-Biodiesel Producer Credit of $0.10 per gallon on the first 15 million gallons of biodiesel produced from plants with production capacity below 60 million gallons per year.

Biomass-based diesel (BBD) was not part of the initial biofuels RFS1 mandate under the Energy Policy Act of 2005, but was included as a distinct category in the RFS2 created under EISA of 2007. While most of this mandate is expected to be met using biodiesel, other fuels, including renewable diesel,[58] algae-based diesel, or cellulosic diesel, would also qualify.

Starting in mid-2007, the U.S. biodiesel industry suffered from unfavorable market conditions as prices for vegetable oil rose relative to diesel fuel (the monthly average wholesale price for soybean oil in Decatur, Illinois, hit $0.62/lb. in June 2008, implying a per-gallon cost of $4.65 for biodiesel). Most biodiesel plants continued to operate into 2008 in hopes of either higher diesel prices or lower vegetable oil prices, and the industry produced then-record output of an estimated

---

[57] See section "The Ethanol Industry's Perfect Storm in 2005."

[58] While similar to "biodiesel," "renewable diesel" is produced through different processes and results in a fuel with somewhat different chemical characteristics. There is a separate tax credit of $1.00 per gallon for renewable diesel.

678 million gallons (**Figure 9**).[59] However, the financial crisis of late 2008 and the ensuing economic recession weakened demand for transportation fuel, and petroleum prices (including diesel fuel) fell sharply in the second half of 2008.

Figure 9. Annual U.S. Bio-Based Diesel (BBD) Production, 1999 to 2022

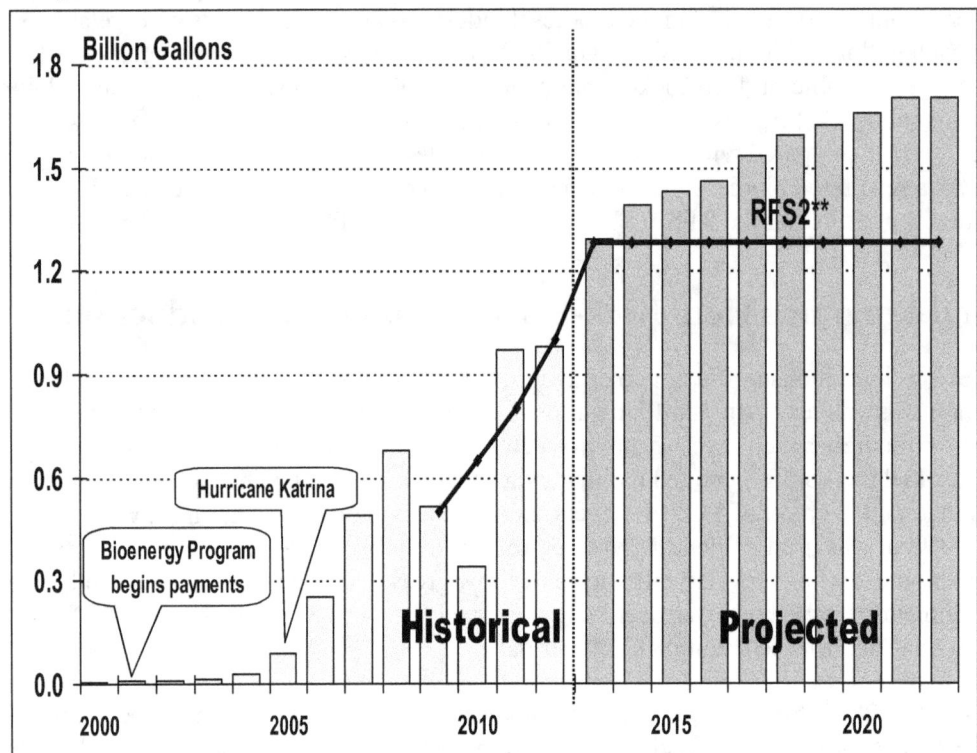

Source: Data for 1999-2012, Energy Information Agency, DOE. Projections for 2013-2022 are from FAPRI, *FAPRI-MU Biofuel Baseline*, FAPRI-MU Report #02-13, March 2013. FAPRI projections assume that market conditions, driven in part by the RFS for advanced biofuel, result in BBD consumption above the RFS for BBD.

Notes: RFS2** shown in the chart represents the RFS for BBD. Although the RFS2 mandate for biodiesel was to begin in 2009, implementation rules were not available until February 2010. As a result, the RFS2 mandate for 2009 of 500 million gallons was combined with the 2010 mandate of 650 million gallons for a one-time mandate of 1.15 billion gallons in 2010. In 2011, the mandate returned to its original trajectory of 800 million gallons, rising to 1 billion gallons in 2012. Starting in 2013, EPA is directed to establish the BBD RFS at no less than 1 billion gallons through a future rulemaking. In its 2013 RFS proposal, EPA proposed a BBD RFS of 1.28 billion gallons.[60] FAPRI assumes that it remains at that level through FY2022.

Starting in 2007 and 2008, U.S. biodiesel producers (relying heavily on the $1/gallon production tax credit) were able to take advantage of a favorable price relationship vis-à-vis the European Union (EU)—which also had domestic policies that encouraged biodiesel consumption—and profitably exported substantial volumes of U.S.-produced biodiesel to the EU. As a result, U.S. biodiesel exports soared to a record 677 million gallons in 2008. However, in March 2009, the EU imposed anti-dumping and countervailing duty tariffs on imports of U.S. biodiesel that effectively shut down U.S. biodiesel exports to the EU and cut in half a major supply outlet for U.S. biodiesel producers (**Figure 10**).[61]

---

[59] DOE, EIA, *Monthly Biodiesel Production Report*, March 2009.

[60] EPA, "EPA Proposes 2013 Renewable Fuel Standards," EPA-420-F-13-007, January 2013.

[61] "EU Imposes Five-Year AD, CVD Duties on U.S. Biodiesel," *Inside U.S. Trade*, July 7, 2009.

Figure 10. Annual U.S. Biodiesel Exports and Imports Since 2001

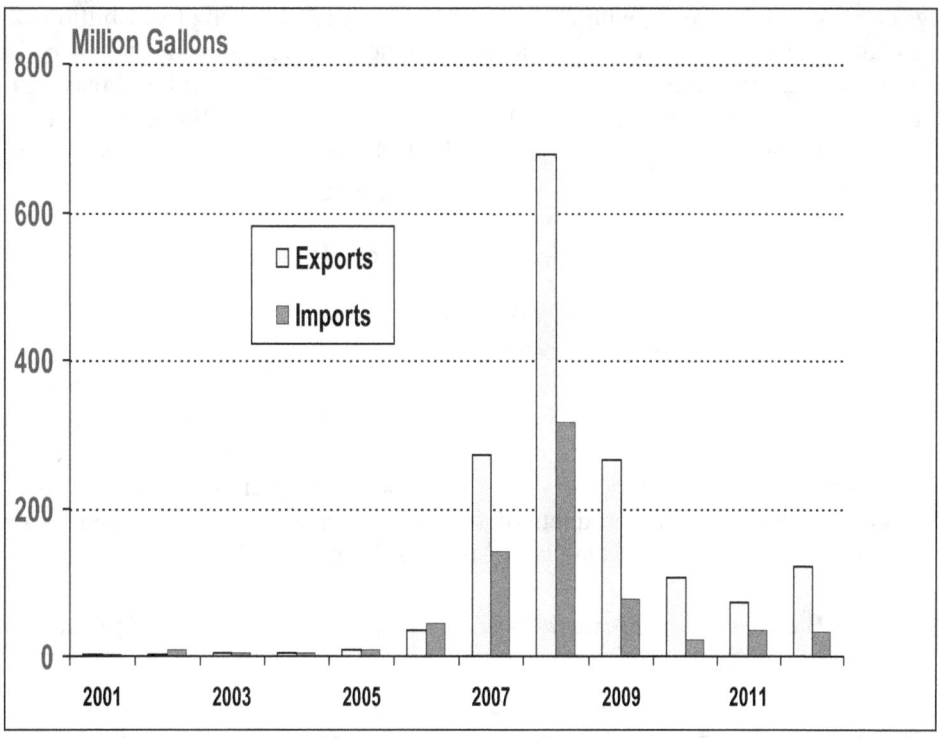

Source: EIA, *Monthly Energy Review*, March 2013, Table 10.4 "Biodiesel Overview."

As a result, the U.S. biodiesel industry experienced several bankruptcies and some loss of capacity during 2009. U.S. biodiesel production in 2009 fell to 516 million gallons, down 24% from 2008.[62] The unfavorable economic conditions for biodiesel production extended into 2010 and were made worse by the expiration of the biodiesel tax credit at the end of 2009. The tax credit was eventually renewed on December 17, 2010 (P.L. 111-312), and made available retroactively to all 2010 biodiesel production; however, the extended delay and poor market conditions contributed to substantially reduced U.S. biodiesel production of 343 million gallons in 2010. During 2010, the U.S. biodiesel industry saw 52 out of 170 operating plants stop operations while many others scaled back on production.[63] The renewal of the tax credit and the expanded RFS2 biodiesel usage mandate of 800 million gallons in 2011 revived the industry and spurred record production of 967 million gallons in 2011 (**Figure 9**).

Once again both the biodiesel tax credit ($1.00/gallon) and the small agri-biodiesel producer credit ($0.10/gallon on the first 15 million gallons) expired at the end of 2011, but were extended through 2013 by P.L. 112-240, which retroactively applied the extension to fuel produced in 2012. In addition to the retroactive tax credit, biodiesel production in 2012 was supported by the RFS2 biodiesel mandate, which grew to 1 billion gallons in 2012. U.S. biodiesel production eclipsed the previous year's record with an output of 969 million gallons in 2012.

Two factors are expected to support biodiesel production at or above 1.28 billion gallons starting in 2013 and going forward: first, the RFS2 biodiesel mandate for 2013 has been proposed at 1.28

---

[62] EIA, *Monthly Energy Review*, March 2013, Table 10.4 "Biodiesel Overview."

[63] "Tax Credits, Mandates Bring Back Biodiesel Plants," *Energy & Environmental New*, September 19, 2011.

billion gallons by EPA; second, the RFS2 for advanced biofuels (for which biodiesel is a qualifying fuel) grows even faster, with 2.75 billion gallons in 2013 rising to 21 billion gallons by 2022. Although cellulosic biofuel was originally envisioned to fill most of the advanced biofuel mandate, slow progress in commercial production to date suggests that biodiesel may be used to meet at least a portion of the advanced biofuel mandate in the future. If this projected outcome were to be realized, it would likely have a profound impact on vegetable oil markets, as biodiesel production would be expected to consume an increasingly larger share of available supplies.[64]

Biodiesel Production Capacity Spreads Nationwide

As mentioned earlier, the primary feedstock for biodiesel includes both vegetable oils and animal fats, both of which are produced over a greater geographic area than corn. As a result, biodiesel plants are more widely dispersed across the United States than are ethanol plants (**Table 3**). As of January 2013, there were 110 companies in the United States with the potential to produce biodiesel commercially that were either in operation or idled, with total annual production capacity (within the oleo-chemical industry) of 2.1 billion gallons per year. Because many of these plants also can produce other products such as cosmetics, estimated total capacity (and capacity for expansion) is far greater than actual biodiesel production.

Table 3. U.S. Biodiesel Production Capacity Partial Estimate as of January 2013

Rank	State	# of Plants	Production Capacity (MGY)	% of Output	Cumulative % output
1	Texas	11	408	20%	20%
2	Iowa	8	250	12%	32%
3	Missouri	8	170	8%	40%
4	Illinois	5	166	8%	48%
5	Washington	4	109	5%	53%
6	Minnesota	4	107	5%	58%
7	Mississippi	3	105	5%	63%
8	Indiana	2	104	5%	68%
9	Pennsylvania	6	90	4%	72%
10	Arkansas	3	85	4%	76%
11	N. Dakota	1	85	4%	80%
12	Kentucky	5	68	3%	84%
13	Ohio	3	67	3%	87%
14	California	9	57	3%	90%
15	Alabama	2	49	2%	92%
	Others (22)	36	168	8%	100%
U.S. Total		**110**	**2,086**	**100%**	

Source: U.S. EIA, "Table 4. Biodiesel Producers and Production Capacity by State, January 2013," *Monthly Biodiesel Production Report*, March 28, 2013.

---

[64] Robert Wisner, "Feedstocks Used for U.S. Biodiesel: How Important is Corn Oil?" *AgMRC Renewable Energy & Climate Change Newsletter*, April 2013; at http://www.agmrc.org.

The unfavorable economic conditions of 2009 and 2010, coupled with the delays in extending the biodiesel tax credit first in 2010 and then again in 2012, and finally the run-up in soybean and product prices in 2011 and 2012, all contributed to a substantial shake-up in the biodiesel industry. Many plants situated in the heart of corn and soybean country dropped out of business, while new plants sprang up in locations near alternate vegetable or animal oil sources. As a result, the U.S. biodiesel industry is more diversified and less centralized than the ethanol industry. Unlike ethanol, where the top six producing states account for 75% of national capacity, the top six biodiesel-producing states achieve only a 58% share, thus demonstrating the more widespread nature of U.S. biodiesel production capacity.

U.S. Transportation Fuel Infrastructure

A key determinant of the demand for biofuels as a transportation fuel is the size and fuel economy of the U.S. vehicle fleet, and the adequacy of the infrastructure (e.g., pipelines, storage tanks, service pumps) that delivers transportation fuel to consumers at the retail level. According to the Department of Energy (DOE), 73% of U.S. transportation fuel is consumed as gasoline or gasoline blends (**Figure 1**), with the remainder consumed as diesel fuel. Gasoline blends and diesel fuel, for the most part, require different infrastructure for delivery to the retail market. In addition, vehicle motors are designed to operate with either gasoline or diesel, but not both.

U.S. Vehicle Fleet

The U.S. Department of Transportation (DOT) estimated that there were 250.2 million registered passenger vehicles (including trucks, buses, and motorcycles) in the United States in 2011, down slightly from 254.2 million in 2009.[65] Included in the fleet of passenger vehicles are more than 14 million flex-fuel vehicles (FFVs), which are capable of operating on the standard 10% ethanol and 90% gasoline (E10) blends as well as higher ethanol blends up to 85% ethanol and 15% gasoline (E85).[66]

Gasoline-Blend Infrastructure Issues

Because of its physical properties, pure ethanol cannot be used in the same infrastructure used to deliver retail gasoline. Nor can ethanol be used in standard automobile engines at high blend ratios, because ethanol tends to make the engine run at a higher temperature than standard reformulated gasoline. In addition, the presence of ethanol can be corrosive on rubber and plastic parts in the car engine. In contrast, biodiesel is very similar in nature to petroleum diesel and does not have the same infrastructure limitations.

The Blend Wall and Higher-Level Ethanol Blends

Prior to October 2010, the amount of ethanol that could be blended in gasoline for use in standard vehicle motors without modification was limited to 10% by volume (E10), by guidance

---

[65] Federal Highway Administration, U.S. Deptartment of Transportation, "State Motor-Vehicle Registration—2011," March 2013, at http://www.fhwa.dot.gov/policyinformation/statistics/2011/pdf/mv1.pdf.

[66] Renewable Fuel Association, "E85," at http://www.ethanolrfa.org/pages/e-85.

developed by the EPA under the Clean Air Act, and certification procedures for fuel-dispensing equipment. In addition, most vehicle warranties did not cover any motor damage resulting from use of ethanol blends above 10%. In the past, only flex-fuel vehicles (FFVs) have been capable of using higher ethanol blends.

As a result, this 10% blend has represented an upper bound (sometimes referred to as the "blend wall") to the amount of ethanol that can be introduced into the gasoline pool.[67] If most or all gasoline in the country contained 10% ethanol, this would allow only for roughly 13 billion gallons, far less than the RFS mandates for 2013 onward.

For ethanol consumption to exceed the so-called blend wall and meet the RFS mandates, increased consumption at higher blending ratios is needed. For example, raising the blending limit from 10% to a higher ratio such as 15% or 20% would immediately expand the "blend wall" to somewhere in the range of 20 billion to 27 billion gallons. The U.S. ethanol industry is a strong proponent of raising the blending ratio.

The blend wall problem is made more acute by substantial revisions in EIA's projections of U.S. transportation fuel consumption rates since the RFS was first passed into law in 2007 (**Figure 11**). At that time, EIA estimated that U.S. transportation consumers were using about 145 billion gallons of gasoline (including ethanol) per year, but that consumption would grow strongly to 176 billion gallons of gasoline by 2022—as a result, RFS mandated biofuels would represent about 19% of annual gasoline consumption. By 2013, EIA had substantially lowered its fuel consumption outlook—partly due to sustained high petroleum prices, the prolonged effects of the 2008 financial crisis on consumer incomes, and significantly higher fuel economy standards on new vehicles. Instead of growth, EIA projects gasoline consumption to fall to about 120 billion gallons by 2022, thus causing the RFS mandate's share of the gasoline transportation fuel market to grow to nearly 20% of annual consumption (in gasoline-equivalent gallons).[68]

EPA Ruling on the Ethanol-to-Gasoline Blending Limit: 10% vs. 15%

On March 6, 2009, Growth Energy (on behalf of 52 U.S. ethanol producers) applied to the EPA for a waiver from the then-current Clean Air Act E10 limit and an increase in the maximum allowable concentration to 15% (E15). After substantial vehicle testing, the EPA issued, first a partial waiver (October 2010) for gasoline that contains up to a 15% ethanol blend (E15) for use in model year 2007 or newer passenger vehicles (including cars, SUVs, and light pickup trucks).[69] Then after further testing, on January 21, 2011, EPA expanded the eligible passenger vehicle pool to include model years 2001 through 2006.[70]

---

[67] CRS Report R40445, *Intermediate-Level Blends of Ethanol in Gasoline, and the Ethanol "Blend Wall"*.

[68] Data is from EIA/DOE's 2013 Annual Energy Outlook. EIA also projects the U.S. national biodiesel transportation fuel market to show slow but steady growth (at about 1% per year) from about 47 bgals in 2012 to nearly 54 bgals by 2022. As a result, RFS BBD's share of the biodiesel transportation fuel market is projected to remain steady at about 2.5% through 2022.

[69] EPA, Fuels and Fuel Additives, "EPA Announces E15 Partial Waiver Decision and Fuel Pump Labeling Proposal," EPA420-F-10-054, October 13, 2010; at http://www.epa.gov/otaq/regs/fuels/additive/e15/420f10054.htm.

[70] See EPA, "E15 (a blend of gasoline and ethanol)," at http://www.epa.gov/otaq/regs/fuels/additive/e15/.

Figure 11. Ethanol Blend Wall Projections, 2007 vs. 2013

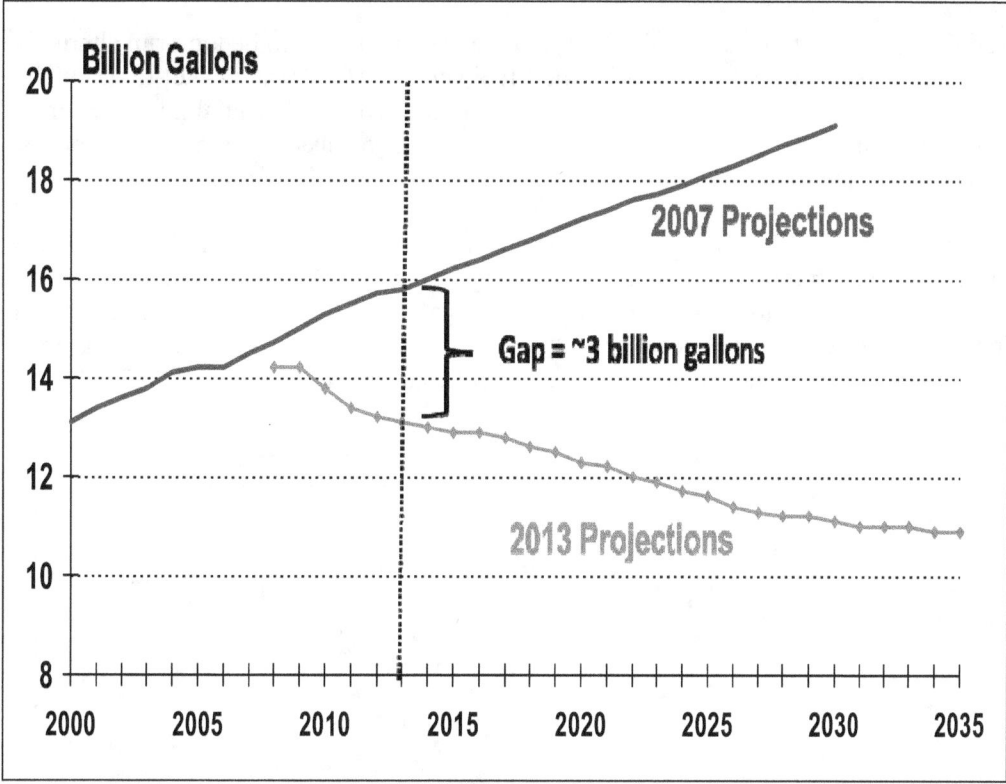

Source: Calculations are by CRS based on data from EIA, DOE, *Annual Energy Review* 2007 and *Annual Energy Review* 2013.

Notes: The blend wall is calculated as a simple 10% share of projections for U.S. gasoline consumption.

However, EPA also announced that no waiver would be granted for E15 use in model year 2000 and older light-duty motor vehicles, as well as in any motorcycles, heavy duty vehicles, or non-road engines. This later restriction opens up the possibility of "mis-fueling"—that is, using higher ethanol blends in vehicles not appropriate for the EPA 15% blend waiver.[71] According to the Renewable Fuel Association (RFA), the approval of E15 use in model year 2001 and newer passenger vehicles covered 62% of passenger vehicles on U.S. roads at the end of 2010.[72]

These EPA rulings would appear to have expanded the eligible vehicle pool for ethanol blends greater than 10%. However, two factors prevent a blend wall expansion to 15%. First, U.S. automakers have not yet extended vehicle warranties to cover any motor damage resulting from use of ethanol blends above 10%. Second, the fact that a portion of currently active passenger vehicles are not eligible for E15—i.e., model year 2000 or older—both limits ethanol retail delivery opportunities and raises the cost of delivery, thus inhibiting retailer adoption.

---

[71] For more information on potential misfueling, see CRS Report R40155, *Renewable Fuel Standard (RFS): Overview and Issues*

[72] "E15 Decision Opens Blend to 2 Out of 3 Vehicles; More Work Yet to be Done," RFA news release, Jan. 21, 2011.

Alternate Options to the Blend Wall

Two additional options to resolving this bottleneck exist, but appear to be long-run alternatives. The first is to increase the use of ethanol in flex-fuel vehicles (FFVs) at ethanol-to-gasoline blend ratios as high as E85. However, increased E85 use would involve substantial infrastructure development, particularly in the number of designated storage tanks and E85 retail pumps, as well as a further expansion of the FFV fleet to absorb larger volumes of ethanol.

According to the Renewable Fuels Association (RFA), more than 14 million FFVs were on the roads in 2012, representing over 5% of U.S. passenger vehicles. However, not all FFV owners have access to (or choose to use) E85 retail pumps. As of early 2013, over 3,000 retail stations in the United States offered E85 (2% out of 142,000 stations).[73] Most E85 fueling stations are concentrated in the midwestern states near the current ethanol production heartland (**Figure 12**).

Figure 12. E85 Refueling Locations by State

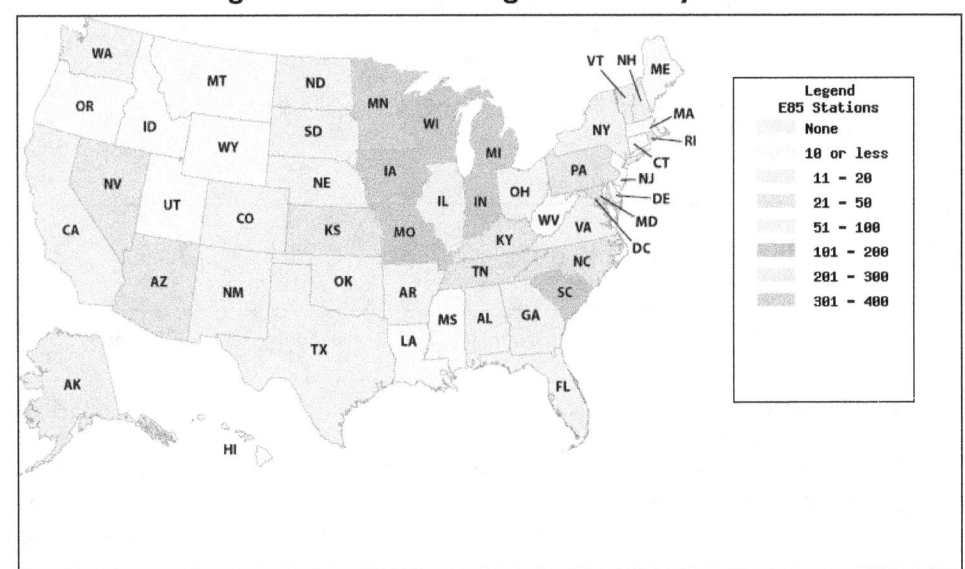

Source: U.S. DOE, Alternative Fuels and Advanced Vehicles Data Center, November 2010, available at http://www.afdc.energy.gov/afdc/ethanol/ethanol_locations.html.

In addition, at blend ratios above 10%, ethanol must compete directly with gasoline as a transportation fuel. For ethanol to operate primarily as a gasoline substitute, it must be priced competitively with gasoline on an energy-content or miles-per-gallon basis.

A second alternative is to expand use of processing technologies at the biofuel plant to produce biofuels in a "drop-in" form (e.g., butanol) that can be used by existing petroleum-based distribution and storage infrastructure and the current fleet of U.S. vehicles. However, more infrastructure-friendly biofuels generally require more processing than ethanol and are therefore more expensive to produce.

---

[73] For more information, see the Renewable Fuels Association's E-85 online information site at http://www.ethanolrfa.org/pages/e-85.

Federal Programs That Support Biofuels

Federal Biofuels Policies Have Encouraged Rapid Growth ...

Federal biofuels programs have proven critical to the economic success of the U.S. biofuels industry, primarily ethanol and biodiesel, whose output has grown rapidly in recent years. Initially, federal biofuels policies were developed to help kick-start the biofuels industry during its early development, when neither production capacity nor a market for the finished product were widely available. Federal policy played a key role in underwriting the initial investments in biofuels production capacity as well as in helping to close the price gap between biofuels and cheaper petroleum fuels.

During the rapid growth period of 2006-2011, U.S. biofuels production and supporting federal budget outlays grew concomitantly. Federal support for biofuels production peaked in 2011, when an estimated $7.7 billion of direct support—including tax credit expenditures ($7.3 billion) and 2008 farm bill Title IX outlays (approximately $300 million)—was incurred.[74] Federal outlays in 2012 are estimated sharply lower, at about $1.3 billion, due to the expiration of several biofuels tax credits.

... And Conflicting Viewpoints

The trade-offs between benefits to farm and rural economies, as opposed to large federal budget costs and the potential for unintended consequences, have led to emergence of both proponents and critics of the government subsidies and mandates that underwrite biofuels production. Oversight and implementation of federal biofuels policies is spread across several government agencies, but the primary responsibility lies with EPA, USDA, and DOE. As the number, complexity, and budgetary implications of federal biofuels policies have grown, so too has the number of proponents and critics.

Proponents of government support for agriculture-based biofuels production have cited national energy security, reductions in greenhouse gas emissions, and raising domestic demand for U.S.-produced farm products as viable justifications. In many cases, biofuels are more environmentally friendly (in terms of emissions of toxins, volatile organic compounds, and greenhouse gases) than petroleum products. In addition, proponents argue that rural, agriculture-based energy production can enhance rural incomes and expand employment opportunities, while encouraging greater value-added for U.S. agricultural commodities.[75]

In contrast, critics argue that, in the absence of subsidies, current biofuels production strategies can only be economically competitive with existing fossil fuels at much higher petroleum prices, or if significant improvements in existing technologies are made or new technologies are developed.[76] Until such technological breakthroughs are achieved, critics contend that the

---

[74] Based on CRS calculations using EIA and USDA data.

[75] Examples of ethanol policy proponents include the Renewable Fuels Association (RFA), the National Corn Growers Association (NCGA), and Growth Energy. Biodiesel proponents include the American Soybean Association and the National Biodiesel Board.

[76] Advocates of this position include free-market proponents such as the Cato Institute, federal budget watchdog groups (continued...)

subsidies distort energy market incentives and divert research funds from the development of other renewable energy sources, such as solar or geothermal, that offer potentially cleaner, more bountiful alternatives. Still others question the rationale behind policies that promote biofuels for energy security. These critics question whether the United States could ever produce sufficient feedstock of starches, sugars, or vegetable oils to permit biofuels production to meaningfully offset petroleum imports.[77] Critics from the petroleum industry argue against the economic costs associated with the imposition of biofuels blending requirements.[78] Finally, some (particularly environmental watchdog groups) argue that the focus on development of alternative energy sources undermines efforts for greater conservation to reduce energy waste.

Many biofuels-related policy debates occur along geographic lines. For example, Midwest corn- and ethanol-producing states are major proponents of federal policy support, whereas many residents of the East and West Coast urban states perceive expensive biofuel usage mandates as being forced upon them while their access to cheaper Brazilian sugar-cane ethanol was, for many years, limited by an import tariff. Another source of biofuels policy conflict has emerged between the major users of corn. Livestock producers have seen their feed costs escalate with the growth in biofuels corn demand and are highly critical of further federal biofuels support.

Federal Biofuels Programs Described

Most of the biofuels policies developed and funded by Congress are subject to oversight and periodic reauthorization.[79] For most of the past three decades, three types of federal programs have provided the core support for the U.S. biofuels industry: blending and production tax credits to lower the cost of biofuels to end users, an import tariff to protect domestic ethanol from cheaper foreign-produced ethanol, and volume-specific usage mandates to guarantee a market for biofuels irrespective of their cost. In addition, the biofuels industry has been supported by several indirect policies in the form of research grants to stimulate the development of new technologies, and grants, loans, and loan guarantees to facilitate the development of biofuels feedstocks as well as market and distribution infrastructure.

Tax Credits

Various tax credits and other incentives have been available for the production, blending, and/or sale of biofuels and biofuel blends (**Table 4**). Tax credits vary by the type of fuel and the size of the producer. Because of their budgetary cost, the tax credits are rarely extended for more than a year or two at a time. As a result, they routinely require congressional action to be extended. On December 31, 2011, most biofuels blending and production tax credits expired, with the exception of the cellulosic biofuels production tax credit, which was set to expire at the end of

---

(...continued)

such as Citizens Against Government Waste, Taxpayers for Common Sense, and farm subsidy watchdog groups such as the Environmental Working Group.

[77] For example, see James and Stephen Eaves, "Is Ethanol the 'Energy Security' Solution?" editorial, Washingtonpost.com, October 3, 2007; or R. Wisner and P. Baumel, "Ethanol, Exports, and Livestock: Will There be Enough Corn to Supply Future Needs?," *Feedstuffs*, no. 30, vol. 76, July 26, 2004.

[78] For example, the American Petroleum Institute (API) and the American Fuel & Petrochemical Manufacturers (AFPM) have brought legal challenges against certain aspects of federal biofuels programs.

[79] For a more complete list of federal biofuels incentives, see CRS Report R40110, *Biofuels Incentives: A Summary of Federal Programs*.

2012. The American Tax Payer Relief Act of 2012 (P.L. 112-240) extended both the producer and small producer tax credits for biodiesel, renewable diesel, and cellulosic biofuels through 2013 and retroactively for 2012.

Table 4. Federal Tax Credits Available for Qualifying Biofuels

Biofuel	Tax Credit: $/gallon	Details	Expiration Date
Volumetric Ethanol Excise Tax Credit (VEETC)	$0.45	Available in unlimited amount to all qualifying biofuels.	Expired Dec. 31, 2011
Small Ethanol Producer Credit	$0.10	Available on the first 15 million gallons (mgal) of any producer with production capacity below 60 mgal.	Expired Dec. 31, 2011
Biodiesel Tax Credit	$1.00	Available in unlimited amount to all qualifying biodiesel.	Dec. 31, 2013[a]
Small Agri-Biodiesel Producer Credit	$0.10	Available on the first 15 mgal of any producer with production capacity below 60 mgal.	Dec. 31, 2013[a]
Renewable Diesel Tax Credit	$1.00	Available in unlimited amount to all qualifying biodiesel.	Dec. 31, 2013[a]
Credit for Production of Cellulosic and Algae-Based Biofuel[b]	$1.01	Available in unlimited amount to all qualifying biofuels.	Dec. 31, 2013[a]

Source: CRS Report R42566, *Alternative Fuel and Advanced Vehicle Technology Incentives: A Summary of Federal Programs.*

a. The tax credit originally expired at the end of 2009 and was not extended until the passage of P.L. 111-312, which retroactively applied the extension to fuel produced in 2010. The tax credit also expired at the end of 2011 and was extended through 2013 by P.L. 112-240, which retroactively applied the extension to fuel produced in 2012.

b. P.L. 112-240, amended the credit to included non-cellulosic fuel produced from algae feedstocks.

Import Tariff on Foreign-Produced Ethanol

Prior to 2012, most imported ethanol was subject to a most-favored-nation duty set of $0.54 per gallon of ethanol (for fuel use) and a 2.5% ad valorem tariff. The stated goal of the import tariff was to offset the ethanol blending tax credit which was also available for foreign-produced ethanol. However, the fixed $0.54-per-gallon most favored-nation duty (identified by 9901.00.50 and 9901.00.52 of the Harmonized Tariff System (HTS)) expired on December 31, 2011. The 2.5% ad valorem tariff (2207.10.60 of the HTS) does not expire but is permanent until or unless the HTS code itself is changed. In most years the tariff was a significant barrier to direct imports of Brazilian sugarcane ethanol. However, some Brazilian ethanol could be brought into the United States duty-free if it was dehydrated (reprocessed) in Caribbean Basin Initiative (CBI) countries.[80] Up to 7% of the U.S. ethanol market could be supplied duty-free in this fashion; historically, however, ethanol dehydrated in CBI countries has only represented about 2% of the total U.S. market.

---

[80] See CRS Report RS21930, *Ethanol Imports and the Caribbean Basin Initiative (CBI).*

The Renewable Fuel Standard (RFS)[81]

As described earlier, the RFS requires the blending of renewable fuels (including ethanol and biodiesel) in U.S. transportation fuel.[82] The RFS is administered by EPA. Under the RFS, fuel blenders are required to blend an increasing amount of renewable fuel in the national transportation fuel supply. This requirement increases annually from 9 billion gallons (bgals) in 2008 to 36 bgals in 2022, of which only 15 bgals can be ethanol from corn starch. The remaining 21 bgals are to be so-called "advanced biofuels"—fuels produced from non-corn-starch feedstocks—of which 16 bgals are to be from cellulosic biofuels, 1 bgals from biomass-based diesel, and 4 bgals from other biofuels (most likely imported sugar-cane ethanol from Brazil). Qualifying biofuels must meet explicit criteria on lifecycle greenhouse gas (GHG) emissions[83] and feedstock production pathways (including restrictions on the land on which feedstocks are produced, feedstock production methods, and the biofuels plant processing technology).

Other Indirect Federal Policies

Several additional biofuels programs have been created to provide various grants, loans, and loan guarantees in support of research and development of related technology, as well as support for biofuels infrastructure development. Many of these programs reside in the energy title (Title IX) of the 2008 farm bill (P.L. 110-246).[84] Federal programs also require federal agencies to give preference to bio-based products in purchasing fuels and other supplies. Cellulosic plant investment is further facilitated by a special depreciation allowance created under the Tax Relief and Health Care Act of 2006 (P.L. 109-432).[85] Also, several states have their own incentives, regulations, and programs in support of renewable fuel research, production, and use that supplement or exceed federal incentives.[86]

In addition to direct and indirect biofuels policies, the U.S. biofuels industry benefits from U.S. farm programs in the form of price and income support programs (i.e., marketing loan benefits and the counter-cyclical payment program) and risk-reducing farm programs (e.g., Acreage Crop Revenue Election (ACRE), Supplemental Revenue Assistance Payments (SURE), federal crop insurance, and disaster assistance), which encourage greater production and lower prices than would occur in the absence of federal programs in a free-market equilibrium.[87] As a result, agricultural feedstocks are both lower-priced and more abundant than without federal farm

---

[81] RFS (referred to as RFS1) was begun by the Energy Policy Act of 2005, (§ 1501; P.L. 109-58). The RFS was greatly expanded (referred to as RFS2) by the Energy Independence and Security Act of 2007 (EISA, § 202, P.L. 110-140). For more information on the RFS, see CRS Report R40155, *Renewable Fuel Standard (RFS): Overview and Issues*.

[82] See the earlier section, "The Renewable Fuel Standard (RFS)," for more details.

[83] CRS Report R40460, *Calculation of Lifecycle Greenhouse Gas Emissions for the Renewable Fuel Standard (RFS)*.

[84] CRS Report R41985, *Renewable Energy Programs and the Farm Bill: Status and Issues*.

[85] Originally the allowance was for cellulosic biofuel plant property. However, P.L. 112-240 amended the credit to included plant property used for non-cellulosic fuel produced from algae feedstocks. The special depreciation allowance involves 50% of the adjusted basis of a new cellulosic or algae-based biofuel plant in the year it is put in service, less any portion of the cost financed via tax-exempt bonds.

[86] For more information, see the "Federal & State Incentives & Laws," Alternative Fuels and Advanced Vehicles Data Center, Energy Efficiency and Renewable Energy (EERE), DOE, at http://www.afdc.energy.gov/afdc/laws/.

[87] For more information on U.S. farm programs, see CRS Report RL34594, *Farm Commodity Programs in the 2008 Farm Bill*; CRS Report R40422, *A 2008 Farm Bill Program Option: Average Crop Revenue Election (ACRE)*; CRS Report R40452, *A Whole-Farm Crop Disaster Program: Supplemental Revenue Assistance Payments (SURE)*; and CRS Report R40532, *Federal Crop Insurance: Background* .

---

programs. This helps lower production costs for the U.S. biofuels sector, and makes U.S. biofuels more competitive with foreign-produced biofuels.

Current Biofuels Policy Issues

Most of the federal biofuels tax credit provisions, as well as the import tariff on foreign-produced ethanol, have short legislative lives and require frequent extension. The primary energy-related issue for the next farm bill is the expiration of program authority at the end of FY2013 and the current lack of mandatory funding going forward for all major energy-related provisions of Title IX.[88] In addition, the appearance of substantial redundancy across renewable energy programs at USDA and DOE, the slow development of the U.S. cellulosic biofuels sector, and concerns about the emerging spillover effects of increasing corn use for ethanol production are issues that are likely to emerge during the next farm bill debate.

Pending Congressional Actions

2008 Farm Bill Expiration

Many provisions of the 2008 farm bill expired at the end of FY2012, but were extended through FY2013 by the American Taxpayer Relief Act (ATRA; P.L. 112-240).[89] Authority for Title IX biofuels policy provisions contained in the 2008 farm bill (P.L. 110-246) also were extended through FY2013, and are expected to be reviewed as part of the next farm bill debate.[90] However, all major bioenergy provisions of Title IX—with the exception of the Feedstock Flexibility Program for Bioenergy Producers—have no new mandatory funding in FY2013 under the ATRA farm bill extension. Although most of the bioenergy programs are reauthorized for FY2013, their mandatory funding expired at the end of FY2012. If policymakers want to continue these programs under either the 2008 farm bill extension or in the next farm bill, they will need to pay for the program with offsets.

The 2008 farm bill authorized $1.1 billion in mandatory funding for energy programs, including $320 million for the Biorefinery Assistance Program, $300 million for the Bioenergy Program for Advanced Biofuels, and $255 million for the Rural Energy for America Program (REAP). The Biomass Crop Assistance Program (BCAP) was authorized to receive such sums as necessary (i.e., funding is open-ended and depends on program participation), although Congress eventually put limits on mandatory funding of $552 million in FY2010, $112 million in FY2011, and $17 million in FY2012. None of the major farm-bill energy programs have baseline funding after FY2012. As a result, the federal budget rules require new revenues or offsetting cuts in order to extend them beyond FY2012.

---

[88] Mandatory funding is derived from authorizing legislation and is not subject to annual appropriations.

[89] For details see CRS Report R42442, *Expiration and Extension of the 2008 Farm Bill*.

[90] See CRS Report R41985, *Renewable Energy Programs and the Farm Bill: Status and Issues*.

Cellulosic Biofuels Tax Credit

While most ethanol tax credits and the import duty on foreign fuel ethanol expired on December 31, 2011, the cellulosic biofuel tax credit and the various biodiesel tax credits do not expire until December 31, 2013. Both the cellulosic biofuels and biodiesel industries can be expected to lobby actively for extension of their tax credits. However, a tight federal budget combined with lack of progress in developing commercial production of cellulosic biofuels are likely to work against an extension. At $1.00 per gallon, the biodiesel tax credit is projected to cost at least $1.28 billion in tax expenditures in 2012, whereas the cellulosic biofuels tax credit is projected to cost about $14 million.

Cellulosic Biofuels Feedstock Program: BCAP

Investors have been slow to invest in what so far is a commercially unproven technology—the conversion of cellulosic biomass to biofuels. Development of the cellulosic biofuels industry hinges on the effective use of new feedstocks. The Biomass Crop Assistance Program (BCAP) was created under the 2008 farm bill to facilitate the development of those new feedstocks and kick-start the cellulosic biofuels industry.[91] BCAP (via USDA's CCC) provides financial assistance in two forms: (1) to support the establishment and production of eligible crops for conversion to bioenergy in selected areas, and (2) to assist agricultural and forest land owners and operators with collection, harvest, storage, and transportation (CHST) of eligible material for use in a biomass conversion facility.

While BCAP is in the early stages of implementation, concerns regarding eligibility, funding, and sustainability continue to be discussed. These issues could shape future congressional action on the program in the context of budgetary measures and possible reauthorization in the next farm bill. In particular, BCAP does not include "baseline" budget spending beyond FY2012. Based on current budgetary requirements, the authorizing committees could potentially need to secure offset funding if BCAP were to be reauthorized in the next farm bill. This could prove difficult given tight budgetary constraints and the more recent and higher projections of the program's cost compared to its initial cost estimates.

Proposed Biofuels-Related Bills in the 113th Congress

The current federal biofuels programs continue to inspire strong sentiments from both advocates and detractors. Several Members of Congress have introduced bills that would either strengthen or reduce (and even eliminate) certain features of current programs.

---

[91] See CRS Report R41296, *Biomass Crop Assistance Program (BCAP): Status and Issues.*

Table 5. Selected Biofuels-Related Bills in the 113th Congress

Bill Number	Bill Name	Sponsor	Action
H.R. 550 S. 251	Phantom Fuel Reform Act of 2013	Rep. Gregg Harper Sen. Flake	To amend the RFS to require the cellulosic biofuel requirement to be based on actual production for the Jan.-Oct. period of the preceding year, pro-rated to an annual basis.
H.R. 596	Public Lands Renewable Energy Development Act of 2013	Rep. Paul Gosar	To promote the development of renewable energy on public lands.
H.R. 796	Amendment to the Clean Air Act	Rep. Sensenbrenner	To limit the cellulosic RFS mandate to be not more than 5% or 1 million gallons (whichever is greater) more than the total volume of cellulosic biofuel that was commercially available for the most recent calendar year.
H.R. 875	untitled	Rep. Sensenbrenner	To provide for a comprehensive assessment of the scientific and technical research on the implications of the use of mid-level ethanol blends (e.g., E15).
H.R. 979	Forest Products Fairness Act of 2013	Rep. Thompson	To modify the definition of the term 'biobased product' to more broadly include forest products.
H.R. 1214	Domestic Fuels Protection Act of 2013	Rep. Shimkus	To provide liability protection for claims based on the design, manufacture, sale, offer for sale, introduction into commerce, or use of certain fuels and fuel additives (e.g., E15).
H.R. 1273	Rural Energy Improvement Act	Rep. Welch	To reauthorize and improve the Rural Energy for America Program (REAP).
H.R. 1461	RFS Elimination Act	Rep. Goodlatte	To repeal the RFS program of the EPA.
H.R. 1462 S. 344	RFS Reform Act of 2013	Rep. Goodlatte Sen. Wicker	To prohibit the EPA from approving the introduction into commerce of gasoline that contains greater than 10%-volume ethanol
H.R. 1469	Leave Ethanol Volumes at Existing Levels (LEVEL) Act	Rep. Burgess	To limit expansion of RFS biofuel mandates, to prohibit authorization of ethanol blends greater than 10%.
H.R. 1482	RFS Amendments Act	Rep. Womak	To eliminate corn ethanol requirements under the RFS program
S. 289	Freedom Fuels Act of 2013	Sen. Baucus	To authorize long-term contracts for the procurement of certain liquid transportation fuels for the Dept. of Defense

Source: Legislative Information System of the U.S. Congress.

Notes: This is not meant to serve as a comprehensive list of all energy-related bills, but instead represents a selection of bills deemed (by CRS) most relevant to federal biofuels programs and policies.

Pending EPA Actions

As administrator of the RFS program, the EPA is responsible for identifying renewable fuel production pathways and pathway components that can be used in producing qualifying renewable fuel under the RFS program. The EPA is also responsible for announcing the RFS mandate levels for each year based on an evaluation and determination of the estimated production capacity (both domestic and international) of the various biofuels types. If it appears that the production capacity will be insufficient for a particular biofuel category—e.g., cellulosic biofuels—then EPA may announce a waiver of the original statutory RFS mandate for that category (and possibly other nested categories) to a reduced level. In addition, EPA may entertain RFS waiver petitions regarding potential economic hardship related to meeting a particular RFS mandate category.

Waiver of Mandated Use Requirements

The RFS mandates the use of over 16.55 bgals of biofuels in 2013. The mandate grows to 20.5 bgals of biofuels use by 2015. By 2022, 36 bgals of biofuels must be consumed under the RFS. Each year EPA must review the likelihood of outyear biofuel production meeting or failing to meet required RFS usage levels, and adjust the mandates accordingly. EPA's biofuels standards for each upcoming year are announced on a preliminary basis in the spring of the preceding year, when EPA issues a notice of proposed rulemaking, and on a final basis by November 30 of the preceding year, when EPA issues a final rule.[92]

The EPA has already waived the original RFS2 mandate for cellulosic biofuels for each of the first three years (2010, 2011, and 2012) and has proposed waiving it for a fourth year (2013). The likelihood of future EPA waivers could deter capital investments in the sector and make future waivers become a self-fulfilling prophecy. The likelihood of meeting RFS mandates for traditional biofuels hinges both on the "blend wall" and on the slow emergence of a national infrastructure needed to facilitate the distribution and use of the growing mandated biofuel volumes. Even if the expansion of the blending ratio to 15% for model year 2001 and newer passenger vehicles were to actually occur (presently an unlikely prospect due to infrastructure limitations mentioned earlier), the higher blend wall of approximately 20 to 21 bgals would become a real barrier to expanded biofuels use by 2015.

Estimation of GHG Emission Reductions

Under EISA, EPA is responsible for evaluating whether a renewable fuel meets the specific GHG reduction threshold assigned to its RFS category. Determining compliance with the thresholds requires a comprehensive evaluation of renewable fuels on the basis of their lifecycle emissions.[93] The concept of "lifecycle emissions" encompasses an evaluation of GHG emissions along the entire pathway of a biofuel from the production, harvesting, and marketing of its feedstocks to the processing and distribution of the biofuel, including any significant indirect emissions such as emissions from land uses changes that might result from changes in crop patterns due to the various biofuels incentives (as explicitly required in Section 201, P.L. 110-140).

More specifically, some have expressed a concern that expanded field crop production in the United States for ethanol production has led to commodity price increases that, in turn, have induced increased land cultivation in other countries, and as a result, have increased net global GHG emissions.[94] The measurement of indirect land use changes (ILUC) is necessarily inexact

---

[92] See CRS Report RS22870, *Waiver Authority Under the Renewable Fuel Standard (RFS)*.

[93] For more information, see CRS Report R40460, *Calculation of Lifecycle Greenhouse Gas Emissions for the Renewable Fuel Standard (RFS)*.

[94] Tim Searchinger et al., "Use of U.S. Croplands for Biofuels Increases Greenhouse Gases Through Emissions from Land-Use Change," *Science*, Vol. 319 no. 5867, February 29, 2008, pp. 1238-1240.

because so many potential activities and countervailing forces are involved. As a result, inclusion of ILUC as part of the EPA's lifecycle GHG reduction analysis has been controversial.

Initially, EPA's lifecycle GHG reduction models proved very sensitive to assumptions regarding the extent of indirect land use changes, and suggested that some standard biofuels may not be eligible for inclusion under the RFS. EPA models were updated prior to the final RFS rule (February 2009) using newer data and produced more inclusive results. For example, corn-starch ethanol was determined to achieve a 21% reduction in GHG emissions compared to the gasoline 2005 baseline, thus just surpassing the 20% reduction threshold.[95] EPA models for estimating land use changes and other life-cycle factors involved in GHG emissions are continually re-evaluated as new or better data, methods, or analytical techniques become available. The nature of the future changes to EPA models, and their potential to include or exclude certain biofuels, remains a critical aspect of the RFS mandates and the U.S. biofuels industry's ability to meet the mandates.

Endangerment Findings for Greenhouse Gases (GHGs)

On April 2, 2007, in *Massachusetts v. EPA* (549 U.S. 497 (2007)), the U.S. Supreme Court determined that GHGs are air pollutants covered under Section 202(a) of the Clean Air Act. The Court held that EPA must determine whether or not emissions of GHGs from new motor vehicles cause or contribute to air pollution that may reasonably be anticipated to endanger public health or welfare, or whether the science is too uncertain to make a reasoned decision.[96] This court ruling allows EPA to regulate GHGs without further congressional action, and could bring into play the issue of indirect land use changes, given their alleged GHG emissions effects, which may put all ethanol production in question. On June 11, 2010, a Senate resolution (S.J.Res. 26) that would have blocked EPA from using the Clean Air Act to regulate GHGs was defeated (53-47).[97] Prior to the vote, on June 8, 2010, the White House had issued a statement saying that if S.J.Res. 26 reached the President's desk (i.e., passed both chambers of Congress), President Obama would veto it.

Other Pending or Emerging Biofuels Issues

CARB's LCFS Restriction on Midwestern Ethanol

In January 2007, then-Governor Schwarzenegger established a Low Carbon Fuels Standard (LCFS) by executive order for California.[98] The executive order directed the state's Secretary for Environmental Protection to coordinate the actions of the California Energy Commission, the California Air Resources Board (CARB), the University of California, and other agencies to develop protocols for measuring the "life-cycle carbon intensity" of transportation fuels.

---

[95] "V. Lifecycle Analysis of Greenhouse Gas Emissions;" Regulation of Fuels and Fuel Additives: Changes to Renewable Fuel Standard Program; Final Rule, 40 CFR Part 80, *Federal Register*, March 26, 2010, p. 14786.

[96] For more information see "Endangerment and Cause or Contribute Findings for Greenhouse Gases under Section 202(a) of the Clean Air Act," EPA, at http://www.epa.gov/climatechange/endangerment.html.

[97] DTN Ag Policy Blog, "Senators Face Emissions Test," Chris Clayton, June 9, 2010.

[98] For more information, see "Low Carbon Fuel Standard," California Energy Commission, at http://www.energy.ca.gov/low_carbon_fuel_standard/index.html.

Under the LCFS, CARB proposed reducing emissions of GHGs by lowering the carbon content of transportation fuels used in California. The LCFS established performance standards that fuel producers and importers must meet each year starting in 2011. Unlike the RFS, which groups biofuels into four categories, the LCFS evaluates each fuel on its own demonstrated level of lifecycle GHG emissions. The LCFS requires that biofuels demonstrate lower lifecycle GHG than the fossil fuels that they replace. For corn ethanol, carbon intensity is lowered by using natural gas instead of coal as a processing fuel, substituting biomass for natural gas or coal, and selling DDGS wet instead of dry.[99] For biodiesel and renewable diesel, carbon intensities can be lowered dramatically by using tallow or recycled cooking oils instead of soybean oil.

As part of its LCFS modeling effort, CARB includes an estimate of the indirect land use changes (ILUC) impact of grain-based ethanol. Largely because of the ILUC value assigned to corn-starch ethanol, most midwestern ethanol production did not qualify for use as a transportation fuel under California's LCFS.[100] This result has important implications for how or whether the federal RFS mandates can be met for the nation as a whole, since California is the largest state (39 million people), the largest consumer of gasoline (over 11% of national highway fuel use),[101] and a major ethanol consumer of approximately 1.5 billion gallons annually.[102]

The ILUC inclusion sparked considerable reaction from biofuel proponents because the measurement of indirect cross-country effects can be highly ambiguous.[103] In late 2010, CARB adopted a resolution to integrate the latest ILUC research into the LCFS regulation. On November 9, 2011, CARB published an updated list of CARB-approved biofuel production facilities that included 22 ethanol plants in Iowa, 21 plants in Nebraska, 12 plants in South Dakota, and 11 plants in Minnesota among the 111 newly added biofuel-plant pathways.[104] On November 26, 2012, CARB published a "Final Regulation Order" describing the LCFS compliance schedule and carbon intensity lookup table for various fuel pathways.[105]

---

[99] EIA, "Biofuels Issues and Trends," October 2012, p. 25, at http://www.eia.gov.

[100] For more information see, "Proposed Regulation to Implement the Low Carbon Fuel Standard," Initial Statement of Reasons, Vol. 1, CARB, March 5, 2009, at http://www.arb.ca.gov/fuels/lcfs/lcfs.htm.

[101] Federal Highway Administration, Dept. of Transportation, "U.S. Motor Fule Use- 2011," Table MF-21, February 2013; at http://www.fhwa.dot.gov/policyinformation/statistics/2011/mf21.cfm.

[102] Todd Neeley, "US Scientists Demand Revision of Biofuels Carbon Accounting," DTN Ethanol blog, May 25, 2010.

[103] A 2010 analysis from Purdue University concluded that CARB overestimated the ILUC impact of grain-based ethanol by a factor of two in developing its LCFS: "New Study Undercuts California Low Carbon Fuel Standard, Shows Evolving Land Use Change Debate," Renewable Fuels Association (RFA), news entry, April 28, 2010, at http://www.ethanolrfa.org. The final version of the Purdue study was released as Wallace E. Tyner, Farzad Taheripour, Qianlai Zhuang, Dileep Birur, and Uris Baldos, *Land Use Changes and Consequent CO2 Emissions due to US Corn Ethanol Production: A Comprehensive Analysis*," Department of Agricultural Economics, Purdue University, July 2010, at http://www.transportation.anl.gov/pdfs/MC/625.PDF. Researchers at DOE's Oak Ridge National Laboratory (ORNL) concluded that ILUC resulting from expanded corn ethanol production over the past decade has likely been minimal to zero: RFA, "Dept. of Energy Researchers: ILUC Impact 'Minimal to Zero,'" 2010 press releases, October 20, 2010, at http://www.ethanolrfa.org; and Debo Oladosu and Keith Kline, ORNL, "Empirical Analysis of the Sources of Corn Used for Ethanol Production in the United States: 2001-2009," presentation to National Corn Growers Association, November 4, 2010; at http://www.ornl.gov/sci/besd/cbes/Symposia/ Empirical_Analysis_Source_Corn_Ethanol_Nov2010.pdf.

[104] CARB, "Fuel Production Facilities with ARB Approved Physical Pathway Demonstrations," LCFS Program, November 9, 2012, at http://www.arb.ca.gov/fuels/lcfs/lcfs.htm.

[105] CARB, "Final Regulation Order (unofficial electronic version)," November 26, 2012, at http://www.arb.ca.gov/ fuels/lcfs/lcfs.htm.

On December 24, 2009, several ethanol groups (including RFA and Growth Energy) filed a lawsuit asserting that the California LCFS violated the U.S. Constitution by seeking to regulate farming and ethanol production practices in the United States under the "commerce clause," which leaves regulation of interstate commerce to the federal government.[106] On December 29, 2011, a U.S. district judge ruled that California's LCFS law did violate the U.S. Constitution's commerce clause and issued an injunction halting enforcement of California's LCFS. The judge ruled that CARB had failed to establish that there are no alternative methods to advance its goals of reducing GHG emissions to combat global warming. After an initial request for a stay of injunction by CARB was denied, a second request for a stay of injunction, while CARB appeals the original ruling, was filed with the Ninth District Court of Appeals and was granted as of April 23, 2012, allowing CARB to continue enforcement of the LCFS until a ruling on the appeal is made.[107]

EU Anti-Dumping Charges Issued Against U.S. Ethanol Exports

U.S. ethanol exports surged to a record 1.2 billion gallons in 2011 (**Figure 7**), driven in part by blending wall limits, but also motivated in part by a sharp fall-off in Brazil's ethanol exports due to high international sugar prices and a below-average sugarcane harvest. The top three destinations for U.S. ethanol exports in 2011 were Brazil (33%), Canada (25%), and the European Union (EU) (24%)—all three of which had their own national biofuels usage mandates. Large U.S. ethanol exports are problematic for two reasons—first, they run counter to the often-cited policy goal of national energy security, and second, they may conflict with biofuels policy goals in other countries, leading to trade disputes.

EU policy has promoted renewable energy use, along with GHG reductions and energy conservation, for much of the past decade.[108] As a result, EU policy support has engendered a substantial domestic renewable energy industry. As part of a "Renewable Energy Directive" adopted by the European Parliament on December 17, 2008, the EU established a 20-20-20 plan that calls for a 20% reduction in GHG emissions compared to 1990 levels, a 20% increase in renewable energy use (with a 10% share specifically in the transport sector), and a 20% reduction in overall energy consumption. As part of the 20-20-20 plan, the EU also adopted a mandate for renewable content in transportation fuels of 5.75% in 2010, rising to 10% by 2020. On October 17, 2012, the EU revised its policy proposal to state that the use of food-based biofuels to meet the 10% renewable energy target in transportation fuels of the Renewable Energy Directive will be limited to 5%.[109]

After the surge of ethanol imports from the United States in 2011, an association of European ethanol producers, ePURE, claimed that the blending tax credit—the $0.45 per gallon incentive known as VEETC—then available to U.S. biofuels blenders represented a subsidy, and that the importation of "subsidized" U.S. ethanol was hurting EU biofuel producers. As a result ePURE requested an anti-dumping (AD) and countervailing duty (CVD) investigation.

---

[106] Todd Neely, "Court Strikes Down California LCFS: Ruling Opens Door to Large Ethanol Market," *DTN: The Progressive Farmer*, December 29, 2011.

[107] EIA, "Biofuels Issues and Trends," DOE, October 2012.

[108] European Commission, "Renewable Energy;" at http://ec.europa.eu/energy/renewables/.

[109] European Commission, "Renewable Energy/Targets by 2020;" at http://ec.europa.eu/energy/renewables/targets_en.htm.

On November 25, 2011, the EU initiated an investigation into whether U.S. exporters sold ethanol at unfair prices and were backed by subsidies in violation of international trade rules to the detriment of EU biofuels producers.[110] At issue is a European allegation that international ethanol traders were exporting E90 (90% ethanol blends) to Europe to take advantage of the EU's lower tariff on such blends as well as the tax incentive for ethanol blending in the United States. In response to the EU anti-dumping investigation, the Renewable Fuels Association (RFA)[111] pointed out that the ethanol tax credits (most of which expired on December 31, 2011) were not made available to U.S. ethanol producers, but "to gasoline blenders, marketers, and other end users."[112]

After a 15-month investigation into a number of U.S. ethanol producers, the EU concluded that U.S. domestic policies aiming to encourage clean energy constitute an illegal subsidy and lead to artificially low-priced imports being "dumped" on the EU market.[113] On February 28, 2013, the European Commission announced that it will impose a five-year anti-dumping duty of 9.5% on all imports of bioethanol from the United States into the 27-nation bloc. In 2009, when similar complaints were lodged against U.S. biodiesel exports, the EU imposed duties of 40% for a five-year period on biodiesel imports originating from the United States.[114]

In response, on April 29, 2013, a bipartisan group of U.S. senators asked the U.S. Trade Representative (USTR), Demetrios Marantis, to investigate the EU decision and consider the possibility of filing a World Trade Organization (WTO) challenge to the European Commission's decision.[115]

The potential implications of an ethanol trade dispute between United States and the EU are unclear. However, the imposition of an import tariff will likely limit U.S. ethanol exports to the EU. Given the emergence of the blend wall as a constraint on U.S. ethanol consumption, combined with relatively tight ethanol supplies on the world market (following two years of successive poor Brazilian sugar crops—2011 and 2012) and biofuels usage mandates in several major fuel consuming nations, the United States may seek international markets for surplus domestic supplies, thus keeping the issue in front of policymakers.

Author Contact Information

Randy Schnepf
Specialist in Agricultural Policy
rschnepf@crs.loc.gov, 7-4277

---

[110] *World Trade Online*, "EU Launches AD, CVD Investigations into U.S. Ethanol Exports," December 8, 2011.

[111] The RFA is a U.S. ethanol

[112] "RFA Responds to EU Ethanol Investigation," RFA News Release, November 28, 2011; http://www.ethanolrfa.org.

[113] International Centre for Trade and Sustainable Development (ICTSD), "Disputes Roundup: Trade Remedies in the Spotlight in Geneva, Brussels," Bridges Weekly Trade News Digest, Vol. 17, No. 7, February 27, 2013.

[114] *Agri-Pulse*, "RFA Tells EU: 'It's Not Us!'" November 30, 2011.

[115] Todd Neely, "Anti-Dumping Questioned," *DTN Progressive Farmer*, April 30, 2013.

www.ingramcontent.com/pod-product-compliance
Lightning Source LLC
Chambersburg PA
CBHW081357170526
45166CB00010B/3116